WORKING ABROAD?

The Guide to Fiscal and Financial Do's and Don'ts

BELIEVE ME, SIR, HAD I SUCH
VENTURE FORTH, THE BETTER
PART OF MY AFFECTIONS
WOULD BE WITH MY HOPES
ABROAD.

Photo: Joe Bates, Jersey.

Harry Brown, dubbed "inimitable" by *The Times,* has been acknowledged as the pre-eminent authority in expatriate affairs. His business and lecturing commitments have taken him to two thirds of the world's countries. In many of them he has broadcast on radio and television. He has contributed innumerable articles to newspapers and other journals and is joint-managing editor of EXPATXTRA! a monthly newspaper-format magazine read by British expatriates in nearly 170 countries of the world.

HARRY BROWN

Northcote House

Four editions of a book of this title written by Harry Brown were previously published by The Financial Times Business Publishing Ltd.

This fifth edition is published by Northcote House Publishers Ltd., Harper & Row House, Estover Road, Plymouth PL6 7PZ.

ISBN 0–7463–0383–1

Typeset and printed by Guernsey Press Ltd., Guernsey, Channel Islands.
Cover design: ADS–Advertising and Design Studios, Jersey, Channel Islands.
Illustrated by Graham Kilwin, Jersey, with apologies to the Bayeux Tapestry.

British Library Cataloguing in Publication Data
Brown, Harry, 1933-
Working abroad? : the guide to the fiscal and
financial do's and don'ts.—5th ed.
1. Alien labor, British—Finance, Personal
I. Title
332.024'00941 HG179

ISBN 0-7463-0383-1

CONTENTS

HERE BE DRAGONS !

PREFACE

I set out to write this revised edition in much the same frame of mind as I wrote the first of the four previous editions nearly a decade ago. Just as I would were I trying to guide you through a stretch of countryside with which I am familiar and in which you might be lost already or in grave danger of being lost.

In each chapter I have tried to remember that I am writing for two audiences; those of you who have been working abroad for some time and those to whom the experience is going to be a whole new ball-game.

A great many changes have taken place in the "landscape" over the years; there has been some planning blight and some downright ugly attempts at conservation but some idyllic spots have been left intact.

I have mapped out the broad, well-trodden highways, encouraged the exploration of some little used footpaths whilst, at the same time, trying to make you aware that there are places where it is foolish and occasionally messy to place your feet. Very often, in preparing the "map" I have been tempted to add the caveat "Here be Dragons", the phrase which old cartographers used when warning travellers when they were uncertain of what dangers, if any, lay in wait.

Having spent a good part of my life writing to, lecturing to and, indeed, very often cringing at the "guts-to-try-anything" attitude of, working British expatriates I think that I know not only where the dangers are but how hot the dragons' breath might be. So I have been more specific than many old cartographers could be: I also know that despite what he might think to the contrary no expatriate is fire-proof.

It is a sad fact of life that many people who go to work abroad, either on secondment to an overseas branch or subsidiary of a UK employer or on contract to a truly overseas company, give less thought to their circumstances than they would if they were simply to be going abroad on holiday for a few weeks.

Most expatriates take far greater care making their holiday arrangements than they do preparing for what may, for many, be the turning point in their careers and financial well-being.

Secondment to an overseas posting is often as the result of the sudden death or sickness of the previous incumbent of the overseas job or it may arise when a particular business venture is entered into or an overseas contract is achieved by the employer.

It is not unknown for an employee to be needed at the other side of the world in a matter of days. Vaccinated, inoculated, visaed, occasionally briefed and always confused the employee climbs into an aeroplane seat to begin a new career. Quite often his family is left behind to fend for themselves for a while; maybe to follow him when circumstances permit; maybe to remain in the United Kingdom while husband and father does several years' work in a country which he has never visited before and to which they will never go.

Faced with such situations it cannot be wondered at that so many expatriates start off on the wrong foot and take little or no advantage of the opportunities which their new life might afford them. If all periods of expatriation began this way, if each intending expatriate had no time to take proper advice, then it might be understandable that such a small number of expatriates make the most of their new status.

It surely cannot be so easily understood if anyone, on secondment or not, goes to work abroad at a more leisurely pace.

Either they as individuals should seek advice or their employers should ensure that they are given it. In either case the expense of such advice is but a drop in the bucket compared to the frightening waste of time, money and effort if, due to his ignorance, the expatriate offends fiscal laws and gets into difficulties.

Taking up a job abroad is a traumatic experience; and not simply for the bread winner. A rational man who would think twice about imposing on his family a change of wallpaper without prior, in-depth consultation, often expects his wife and his children, some of whom might be reaching crucial stages in their own lives, to follow him abroad without question or remain in the United Kingdom without his day to day support. It is not surprising that, in such circumstances, the ambition of many men to work abroad is thwarted by the apparent donkey-like intransigence of their families.

A proper approach to the whole matter should be adopted and that approach should include the realisation that advice is almost invariably needed prior to going to work overseas, throughout the term abroad and before returning to the United Kingdom to resume life there.

"Decide in haste and repent at leisure" is an axiom which is the epitaph of many an expatriate's shattered illusions.

Whilst accepting that there **are** emergency situations, that there **are** occasions in which reason must give way to expedience, it should be stressed that as each migrant worker has unique individual problems the greater time before expatriation that he has to obtain advice the more likely he is to get the greater benefit.

Having found a competent adviser it is in his own interests to continue consultations throughout his period of expatriation.

Real life rarely lives up to the ideal. Many expatriates have gone abroad and continue to be abroad without ever having taken any advice. Some of them survive; just as some unattended plants survive in a garden. But do the majority bear the fruit they promised? Not usually without receiving some help.

Each month the mail-bag of EXPATXTRA!, of which I am an editor, yields numerous, very sad [and in the main totally avoidable] stories of substantial amounts of UK tax being levied upon some expatriates who misunderstand the rules and have, for years, considered themselves exempt from a liability. Some expatriates who were lured, enticed or encouraged to work abroad by advertisements which promised "tax free" salaries; only to find out the bitter truth that **there is no such thing as a salary that is automatically free of United Kingdom tax however long and however hard the recipient works abroad.**

There is advice to be obtained in plenty. Most banks, investment houses or insurance companies who specialise in providing services to expatriates can help; many publish booklets which will help.

Some publish booklets which will not!

Many insurance and financial advisers now have specialist staff trained to deal in the complexities. It should not be difficult to receive proper counselling provided you are prepared to pay for it either in fees or in the realisation that many advisers rely upon the commission from sales to maintain their services.

There are several journals specifically aimed at the expatriate population; "Resident Abroad", "The Expatriate" and EXPATXTRA! amongst them. An expatriate who subscribes will remain aware of the many financial advisory services available to him and, at the same time, have the chance to read the expert comments of the specialists contributing articles.

It would be true to say that just as there is a vast army of working British expatriates there is a vast army of commentators and advisers willing and able to provide the answer to many of the problems that arise. It would also be true to say that many expatriates expect expert advice without paying for it in one way or the other. Disillusion makes a lumpy mattress.

It is at this point in the preface of most books that the author becomes effusive and lists the names of those without whose contribution he would not have survived the labour-pains of producing the work. I shall be no exception to the golden rule; my mid-wives were very caring.

But before I comply I want to offer an apology, or at least an explanation, to any women expatriates into whose hands this book might fall. You will notice that unless circumstances dictate otherwise I have referred to every working British expatriate as though only men worked overseas. I have done so because the UK tax regulations as they apply to working expatriates take no account of the gender of the person.

Despite what many women expatriates might think the law is the law is the law whether you, the reader, are male or female. To have prefaced every one of my remarks with "his/her, him/she," would have been unwieldy, untidy and unnecessary.

That out of the way I am left room for my acknowledgements. I offer my undiluted gratitude to Catherine Richmond who undertook the task of editing this edition and without whose help the book would have remained on the backs of the envelopes, menus, parking tickets and air sickness bags upon which it was scribbled: my over-worked dictionary for springing to my aid every time I looked at a word and said "that doesn't look right"; to Brian West of Lloyds Bank Plc, here in Jersey, who read the typescript when it was completed and Jack Walder who has offered me advice on each book I have written over the years.

I also particularly want to thank the working expatriate mates of mine who were kind enough to stop doing whatever they were being paid to do and take time out to provide me with an essential sounding board.

Once in a while I have been told that I seem to take delight in being rude about working expatriates in what I write or say on the subject: that I do not offer them the deference they believe is due to them. Perish the thought!

In my travels around and around the world I have been fed, watered and sheltered, startled, annoyed and even angered by expatriates in 140 countries. Hardly the act of a gentleman to allow any of my hosts to read my thoughts from anything that I might say or write; but it could have happened, I suppose.

To make up for any lapses on my part I respectfully dedicate this edition to all working British expatriates everywhere.

Harry Brown
September 1986

PO Box 300
Jersey, Channel Islands

UK TAXATION

The immortal words of Sherlock Holmes sum up the attitude that anyone should adopt when faced with a situation which he does not fully comprehend.

Although the UK tax implications of working abroad can be quite onerous they are not insurmountable provided you think about them hard enough, long enough and clearly enough.

As when trying to resolve any other problem you will find that in all relevant aspects of UK tax it helps to have the basic facts to hand.

The fundamentals affect **every working British expatriate;** there are no exceptions although many expatriates by custom, bad advice or sheer stupidity have assumed that they are beyond the regulations which the UK Revenue administer and administer well.

I shall first set out the fundamentals, enlarge upon their effects and then give you an example or two as to how these basics can apply to a working British expatriate.

The UK Revenue's function and objective is to assess for tax

a] **all income arising in the UK no matter to whom it belongs**

and

b] **all income arising anywhere in the world which belongs to persons resident in the UK.**

There are situations in which these general objectives do not apply. In those circumstances a person's liability can also be determined by what is known as his domicile; in the main those circumstances do not apply to working British expatriates but later I shall touch upon the relevant points of domicile.

The UK taxation aspects upon which the working expatriate needs advice include not only income tax but capital gains and the newly introduced UK inheritance tax too. These too are matters into which I shall also delve later in the chapter; income tax first.

Tax law is regulated by the Inland Revenue so it will be as well that you have in mind some interpretation of certain terms they constantly use. Some of the definitions are my definitions because in some instances the Revenue do not issue definitions; relying on the individual circumstances of an expatriate to determine whether a liability to tax has arisen.

"Tax year" means the UK fiscal year which is the twelve months stretching from April 6th through to April 5th following.

"United Kingdom" comprises only England, Wales, Scotland and Northern Ireland; it does **not** include the Channel Islands or the Isle of Man. These low tax areas are part of Britain but not part of the UK which is, in effect, a tax and excise union.

"Abroad" and **"Overseas"** mean outside the UK.

"Working expatriate" means a person in full time and continuous employment outside the UK; a person who performs all the duties of his employment, other than duties which might be regarded as "*merely incidental*" outside the UK. Duties which might automatically be considered as "*merely incidental*" have not been defined.

The chances of the Revenue ever being so bold as to define them are, at their highest, nil. I shall offer guarded comment as to possible interpretations later.

"Residence and ordinary residence" have not been defined in any UK income tax legislation either. However from time to time some clue to the legal meaning of these words has been given in decisions by the Courts. Hardly earth-shattering clues because they show that both expressions are used in their everyday, common-or-garden sense and have no special or technical meaning. But remember that together the expressions combine to make the scales upon which every expatriate's possible liability to UK tax is weighed.

"Domicile" on the other hand is always used in its strict legal sense.

Income tax legislation and regulations covering employment abroad refer always to **emoluments;** not just the income derived from the employment.

The term **"emoluments"** as used by the Revenue means any kind of reward for doing a job. It includes salaries, fees, bonuses, pay, wages, overtime pay, leave pay, commission, tips, gratuities and foreign cost of living allowances. It also includes any benefit in kind such as travel allowances, school fees, housing provision or the like paid to an employee whose total emoluments are at a rate of £8,500 or more per annum.

It must be apparent that almost all working expatriates fall into this category since few, if any, would work abroad in full time employment for emoluments which do not total £8,500 per tax year.

In Inland Revenue parlance "resident" and "ordinarily resident" are always used to describe a situation arising in a tax year and never refer to some longer or, indeed, shorter period. The question which generally has to be answered for tax purposes is whether a person is resident [or ordinarily resident] in the UK in a particular tax year. Each case depends on its own, peculiar facts. Always remember that.

Never assume because a friend or colleague, working abroad under similar circumstances to you, has been designated as not resident and not ordinarily resident that you will be.

To be regarded as "resident" for UK tax purposes

For anyone to be regarded as resident in the UK for a given tax year he must normally be physically present there for at least part of that year. He will invariably be resident if he is there for six months or more in that year, for whatever purpose. Illness, disability or family crisis is no excuse. There are no exceptions to the rule. Six months is regarded as 183 days whether or not the year in question is a leap year.

For this purpose the total number of days spent in the UK, whether the stay is of one period or a succession of visits, is aggregated to see whether the number of days spent within the UK exceeds 182.

To be regarded as "ordinarily resident" within the UK

To be regarded as ordinarily resident within the UK is broadly equivalent to being habitually, usually, more-often-than-not there. Anyone who is resident within the

UK year after year is considered ordinarily resident there too; as is anyone who averages more than 90 days per tax year in the UK, year after year.

It follows then that most people who live in the UK are both resident and ordinarily resident within the UK before they go abroad to work.

Equally obvious is the fact that the quicker anyone can convince the Revenue that he falls outside the scope of the residential laws the better it will be for him. He will have succeeded in becoming both **not resident and not ordinarily resident** within the UK and **that will mean that the Revenue will no longer have any interest in taxing his overseas emoluments.** Remember however that the Revenue will still have the right to impose UK tax on any assessable income that arises there. The rental income from the letting of the UK home whilst abroad, for example.

Strictly speaking each tax year has to be looked at as an entity and the person has to be treated as either resident or not resident for the whole year; he cannot, normally, be regarded as resident for part of the tax year and not resident for the remainder.

But there is a concession by which the Revenue will "split" the year into periods of residence and non-residence **if a person goes abroad to work in full time and continuous employment for a period which includes a full tax year.** Provided you can assure them that you are going to work abroad for such a period then both the tax year of your departure and the tax year of your permanent return will be split [purely by concession] into periods of residence and non-residence; periods in which you will not be subject to UK tax on your emoluments and periods in which you will.

As you might expect there is a little more than splitting the initial and final tax years to be worried about; you need to be intent on remaining "not resident and not ordinarily resident" for the whole of your period of expatriation; otherwise dire tax consequences can result, as I shall explain.

The regulations which determine this highly-to-be-desired status for a working British expatriate are that **he MUST go abroad for full time employment under a contract of employment** and

a] **MUST perform all the duties of his employment abroad and ensure that any duties he performs within the UK are merely incidental to his overseas duties**

and

b] **his absence from the UK in that employment MUST be for a period which includes at least one full tax year**

and

c] **interim visits to the UK — for whatever purpose — MUST not amount to six months [183 days] or more in any one tax year OR three months [90 days] on average year after year.**

If he adheres to those regulations then from the day **after** he goes abroad to the day **prior** to his return to resume tax residence he will be regarded as not resident and not ordinarily resident within the UK for tax purposes. Given those circumstances he will not be liable to UK tax upon his overseas emoluments.

Right at the beginning of this chapter I warned you that you would have to think long and hard over the many complex regulations which will affect you whilst you are working abroad. What I will say now is that if you think the regulations I have already outlined are complex then "you ain't seen nothing yet"!

But before we go on to look at the complexities let us apply what we already know of the rules to an example.

Alan Able, an engineer, is employed by a Manchester firm; the firm obtain a contract to install a vast quantity of equipment in Dubai and he is asked to go abroad for three years to ensure its correct installation. He is offered a salary of £35,000, and "perks" like housing benefits, education fees for his fourteen-year-old twin sons. His employers tell him that everything will be TAX FREE!

"Fantastic!", thinks Alan.

Although he probably does not realise it his total emoluments package is £100,000 per annum. Housing in Dubai, school fees and allied matters such as air fares are very expensive.

Alan and his wife, Anne, decide that they will not lease out their home whilst abroad. He has no other source of income [such as interest from bank accounts]. They leave the UK on 30th September 1986 and apart from a month-long spell in hospital and normal leave periods he works abroad until his contract ends on 30th September 1989.

Then he returns to the UK to resume his duties there.

A wealthier man, experienced in an overseas assignment; his twin sons having had the benefit of three years private education at no expense to him and his wife. Diagrammatically his period abroad looks like this:

Tax year 1986-87

6.04.86....R & OR.......... 30.9.86......*Provisionally* NR & NOR......... 5.04.87

departure from UK — ***20 days leave in UK***

Tax year 1987-88

6.04.87 ....*Provisionally* NR & NOR.......................... 5.04.88

25 days leave in UK — ***30 days hospitalisation in UK***

Tax year 1988-89

6.04.88 .... NR & NOR.................................. 5.04.89

45 days leave in UK

Note

From 1st October 1986 [the day following his departure] to the end of his first full tax year abroad [5.04.88] Alan will be provisionally not resident and not ordinarily resident for UK tax purposes.

The Revenue will hold him in this provisional "limbo" until 6.04.88 since he will not have actually done what he indicated that he would do; that is "work in

full time employment abroad for a period which includes at least one full tax year".

From 6th April, 1988, until 5th April, 1989, he will be fully not resident and not ordinarily resident since he will have fulfilled his obligations. His having spent time in the UK both on leave and in hospital will not affect his tax status since he did not exceed his allowable time there in any one tax year.

Tax year 1989-90

6.04.89 .... NR & NOR.29.09.89.......R & OR 5.04.90

30 days leave in UK — *Permanent return to UK*

Note

This is the tax year of his permanent return to the UK. Under the concession the year of his return, just as was the year of his departure, will be split into periods of residence and non-residence.

In short Alan Able will pay no UK tax upon his overseas emoluments from the day following his departure to the day preceding his permanent return. Despite his illness a wholly acceptable arrangement as far as he is concerned.

The "splitting" of Alan's tax year of departure and tax year of his permanent return into periods of residence and non-residence is also to his advantage. **For the periods in both years for which he is considered resident for tax purposes he will receive a whole year's personal allowance to set off against his UK tax liabilities.** In the year of his departure [1986-87] since he paid tax under the PAYE system [ie, he received his personal allowances in instalments rather than in a lump sum] Alan will have over-paid tax and can claim it back by completing Inland Revenue form P85 and submitting it to his normal district tax office. In the year of his permanent return [1989-90] he will complete forms P86 and P15 [announcing his return to work in the UK] and receive a whole year's personal allowance to be applied to his UK emoluments between the date of his resuming work and the end of that tax year [5th April 1990].

As soon as he returns to the UK to resume his duties there Alan will be regarded as resident [and probably ordinarily resident too since it is his intention to remain there] for UK tax purposes. From that moment the whole of his future world wide income will be assessable for UK tax, as will any capital gains he might make in the future.

Terminal leave and bonus payments

However, it is not at all unusual for a long term expatriate to be offered some terminal leave from his overseas contract; as sort of "good boy" bonus for completing the overseas contract. Even if Alan receives the payment for that leave whilst in the UK at the end of his overseas contract he will not suffer UK tax upon it. Nor will he suffer tax upon any contract-end bonus paid provided it relates to his services abroad and provided that during his time abroad he was not resident and not ordinarily resident in the UK.

Remittances to the UK

Had Alan been working in a country with restrictive legislation about the exportation of savings [many West African countries have such exchange control complications] he might have found that it took him several months [bad cases take years] to receive savings "blocked" by the foreign country. Provided these monies are from the result of his overseas contract then he will not be subject to UK tax upon them even if, when he eventually receives them, he is resident and ordinarily resident in the UK.

Many expatriates have to leave their wives and families back in the UK whilst they work overseas. Naturally they need to provide normal housekeeping and maintenance payments to the family. Equally naturally many expatriates worry whether such payments from their overseas emoluments should be declared for income tax by the UK-based wife; especially if she is herself in employment in the UK.

Such normal housekeeping payments and, perhaps, other monies sent for household improvements or birthday gifts are not regarded as being part of the recipient spouse's income and therefore will not suffer UK taxation.

UK based working wives

Many women successfully combine running a family with following a career in the UK whilst husbands are working abroad. Prior to his going to work in full time employment overseas the wife and the husband may have elected to be taxed as one person [that is normally the case unless both have reasonably substantial UK incomes]. When the husband becomes not resident and not ordinarily resident for UK tax purposes the UK-based wife will be treated by the Inland Revenue as though the husband did not exist; which, of course, for their purposes he does not. The wife will be regarded as a *femme sole* and receive the appropriate single person's tax allowance to set off against her UK tax liabilities. Once again no housekeeping payments made to her by the husband will be subject to income tax in her hands.

It will be interesting [and, hopefully, instructive] as we progress through this chapter to examine Anne Able's situation and the effects that an infringement of the rules by Alan might have had on the financial outcome of Alan's stint abroad.

Available accommodation

On many occasions a decision as to whether a person can be regarded as resident or ordinarily resident for UK tax purposes hinges upon whether he has "a place of abode" available to him there.

Where this does happen and a person's residence position does turn on whether or not he has available accommodation the question is whether any accommodation is, in fact, available to him for his use. Ownership of the accommodation is immaterial; the Revenue accepts that ownership of the property does not necessarily imply access to it.

An expatriate could own several houses in the UK for investment purposes; they could all be leased to tenants. He owns them but they are not available to him since they are occupied by tenants.

Just as easily accommodation can be said to be "available for the use" of an expatriate when it is owned by someone else.

His parents may have a "Granny flat" or a country cottage which they set aside for his use when he is in the UK. Caravans have been regarded by the Revenue as "a place of abode"; and on one occasion a single bedroom was so designated because the expatriate's wife had a chronic back condition and had left an orthopaedic bed in her Mother's spare room for her use when on leave. Also remember that a house owned or rented by one spouse is usually considered available for the use of the other; a natural, if sometimes, an erroneous assumption.

However, the available accommodation rule is not applied if the person to whom it is available is working full time in a business, profession or employment carried on wholly abroad.

Provided that the working expatriate satisfies all the other conditions to establish himself as neither resident nor ordinarily resident within the UK his having available accommodation during visits to the UK will not destroy his advantageous tax position.

Other expatriates, those not in full time and continuous employment overseas, fall foul of this regulation by the tens of thousands each year. Normally it is the husband who is the working expatriate; often his wife, though living abroad as long as he each year, is unable to work full time. Work permit problems in the overseas country might preclude her from doing so. What then?

Let us return for a while to the example of Alan and Anne Able.

For the whole of the time that Alan worked abroad they left their UK home unoccupied. So, every time that Alan returned on holiday or to go into hospital the house was available to him; just as it was available to Anne.

Because he could claim that he was in full time employment overseas for the requisite amount of time his status remained non-resident. However, Anne, his wife, since she was not in full time employment overseas, breached the rules. Every time she set foot in the UK she became resident for UK tax purposes for the whole of the year in which she went there. She also, undoubtedly, became ordinarily resident there because she went back year after year.

Please remember what I told you earlier; I was anxious to point out that anyone who is regarded as resident year after year is also regarded as being ordinarily resident in the UK too. That would mean that her world wide income and capital gains would remain subject to UK taxation. The "183 day or 90 day average" rule did not catch Anne; the "available accommodation" trap did.

Since she is not working the likelihood is that her being resident and ordinarily resident is more of a technical detail than anything too worrying to the Able's overall financial well-being.

But what if, as is not at all unusual, Alan had designated all his interest-bearing deposit accounts in their joint names? What if any investments he had made were also jointly held by them? Anne will have some income and some capital gains to declare; she will have half of the interest on the bank accounts and half any capital gains that their investments might have earned. It is no matter where in the world the bank accounts or investments were held; **a resident of the UK is taxed on world wide income and world wide capital gains.**

This point is amongst the most upsetting fiscal matters with which non-working expatriate wives have to contend. When a married couple have been used to sharing financial difficulties most of their lives they find it hard not to share the benefits in saving excess income from the husband working overseas. Either a change in philosophy has to be adopted or the potential tax impost has to be recognised.

As a UK tax resident Anne will have been able to claim the personal allowance of a single person [£2,335 for 1986/87] so the tax imposition might not be too great if the joint account was "modest"; but some husbands and wives keep very large amounts of money in jointly held interest bearing accounts. The penalties for doing so can amount to very large amounts of UK tax on the share of the interest which the wife enjoys.

It is essential that you remember that accommodation has only to be available for this trap to be sprung. It does not have to be used for the rule to come into play.

Let us say that during their leave period in 1988-89 [see example] Alan and Anne had decided to spend the whole of their stay visiting friends along the south coast of England. Let us assume that their home is in Manchester. They flew into and out of Heathrow and went direct to their friends. Not once did they move north of Heathrow; they were two hundred or more miles away from Manchester for the whole leave period.

Anne will still have offended the rules since she set foot in the UK at a time when accommodation was available to her. She will be regarded as resident for UK tax for the whole of the tax year 1988-89; just as though she had never left the country.

Please do not imagine that this rule is aimed at women expatriates; that they are its sole target. The rule would apply with equal severity if Anne had been the working expatriate and Alan had simply gone abroad to live there with her instead of it being the other way round. It is just a simple fact of life that most working expatriates are men.

Remember that during his visit to his friends Alan would have had no personal worries about his residential status since he was a working expatriate

a] performing the whole of his duties abroad [apart from incidental ones]
and
b] doing so for a period that included at least one full tax year
and
c] restricting his visits to less than 183 days in any one tax year or 90 days on average year after year.

He will remain not resident and not ordinarily resident for UK tax purposes.

Remember, as well, that until the first full tax year has been spent in overseas employment Alan's status as a non-resident is only provisional. He has actually to fulfil the requirements before his non-resident status can be said to be cast-iron. He may, of course, spend normal leave periods in the UK during that provisional period; his doing so will not be to his detriment provided he does complete the contract and remain working overseas for the required period.

Incidental duties

Earlier in the chapter I undertook to try to give guarded views on what does and what does not constitute duties which can be said to be incidental to the overseas employment. These are duties which can be carried out within the UK and still be regarded as not offending the basic rules I defined earlier that all duties of an overseas employment must be performed outside the UK. Before doing so I issue the caveat that a] these are my views designed to explain examples that I have carefully chosen and b] my views have been known to not coincide with those of the Revenue.

When you are playing ball with the Inland Revenue they have the upper hand since they choose the ball and the game you play with them; and since you may not know all the rules they can shout "foul", blow the whistle and claim a penalty whenever they like. Appealing to the "referee" can be a very expensive exercise so it is best to make sure that you stay well outside the penalty area.

Let us go back to Alan Able and assume that during his first home leave his employers ask him to go to their head office and report of the progress of the contract which he is overseeing. Would his reporting be regarded as a duty which was merely incidental to his overseas duties? Undoubtedly it would be and he would not upset the Revenue's rules.

But what if, during his leave period, his employers had a problem with a technical matter in a contract which they were undertaking in Scotland? What if they thought that Alan, being such an expert, could help them out by visiting the site to give his opinion? That would, assuredly, not be regarded as part of his overseas duties nor incidental to them. Alan would have broken the rules and would pay the tax penalties.

The classic cases which have been brought before the Courts in order to obtain a ruling have invariably been far more glamorous. One of the most celebrated concerned a British pilot who went to work for a foreign airline; part of his duties as the Captain of the aircraft was to land it at Heathrow en route for the United States. The Revenue pounced and said that in their view he was breaking the rules; the Captain said that he was not. They went to the Courts where learned counsel argued in front of an even more learned judge.

Cutting a very long and highly technical story short the Judge indicated that if the Captain considered landing an aircraft at Heathrow as "incidental" then he, the Judge, would not like to be a passenger!

He found for the Revenue; clearly establishing that what the Captain might have thought of as incidental to his main occupation of actually keeping the plane in the air was a "substantial" part of his overseas duties. That landing a plane and flying it were all part and parcel of what he was being paid for and what he had undertaken only to do abroad.

So, taking His Lordship's views as the gospel they are, what would have happened to Alan, if instead of just reporting to his employers, he had spent some time designing equipment or interviewing staff to join him in Dubai? Would interviewing be "incidental"? Would designing equipment not be part of his overseas duties and a substantial one at that? Is that not what engineers do? And should not Alan have done his designing abroad; where he was being paid to do his job?

Please look no further for an answer from me! Dare, if you will, to ask the Revenue, particularly if you have found [or are likely to find] yourself in a similar situation. I am none too confident that you will get a soft answer that turneth away the Revenue's wrath.

On one matter concerning incidental duties I can be specific.

Expatriates holding Directorships of overseas companies are especially vulnerable to breaking the rules; particularly those with the title of Managing Director.

The Revenue has most clearly stated

"There are practically no duties of a Director which can be regarded as purely incidental to other duties. Almost anything a director does on company business is not regarded as a mere incident of something else".

"The words Managing Director have an even greater degree of elasticity and include not only normal direction of subordinates but also a large measure of responsibility for making policy, discussing, advising, receiving and giving information. The office therefore carries with it a variety of duties practically all or which are so substantive in themselves that it is very exceptionally considered that any one duty is merely incidental to some other duty of his".

So, you have been warned. Had Alan been the Managing Director of his firm's overseas company then he most certainly would not have escaped with the plea that he was "only reporting to his superiors back home". He would undoubtedly have been regarded as resident in the UK for tax purposes and his overseas emoluments would have been assessable for UK tax. I shall repeat that; **his overseas emoluments would have been assessable for UK tax.**

Please look back at the example. See that his income was £35,000, **TAX FREE** and that I had an educated guess that by the addition of the various perks such as housing, school fees for his twins etc. his emoluments would total £100,000 a year. That is the sum [and I believe the guess to be on the low side] upon which the Revenue would raise an assessment to income tax; simply because Alan had infringed the rules and performed a duty in the UK which was not incidental to his overseas duties.

The UK tax on £100,000 is almost twice the actual cash that Alan has been earning abroad.

Even if he had saved every penny he had earned he would not have enough to pay the tax bill and yet, you will notice, that in common with many expatriates who go to work in the Middle East, Alan had it indicated to him that the job was **TAX FREE!**

I repeat here what I said in my preface.

No overseas job done by any expatriate carries with it emoluments which are automatically free of UK tax. No job, no how, no where, never!

That is an indisputable fact! I do not care that often you see advertisements from employers offering tax free overseas salaries; I do not care that you might even see totally misleading advertisements for tax free jobs overseas placed in journals by the Manpower Services Commission [a UK Government sponsored agency].

Such advertisements, I believe, should be refused by the journals involved or forced to carry a UK Government Wealth Warning.

In the circumstances I have outlined Alan would have paid UK tax on all his emoluments AND the interest generated by his bank accounts AND realised capital appreciation attributable to his investments; no matter where in the world his savings or investments were placed.

He would have been in exactly the same situation had his illness proved serious and his stay in a UK hospital had been protracted enough either to force him to return home permanently prior to the expiration of his first full tax year abroad or to remain in the UK for so long a time that he breached the 183 day rule.

Enforced early return

Leaving aside the consequences of any performance by Alan of substantive duties within the UK let us consider the equally undesirable happenings in the event that sickness or debility might have had were he to have not completed his scheduled contract.

I do not wish to be considered the spectre at any expatriate's feast but I should be failing in my duty if I did not point out the dramatic events that can take place when an overseas contract of employment is either found to be lacking by reason of duties being performed in the UK or, more likely perhaps, if the contract has to be foreshortened because of serious illness or the inability of the expatriate and his family to cope happily with foreign surroundings.

The same knock-on effect is felt if commercial failure of the contract abroad or political or social unrest makes an evacuation of the foreign country imperative.

The death of an expatriate is the only reason which the Inland Revenue will take as an "excuse" and the only circumstance under which the tax liability will be "forgiven".

Although sympathetic to his problems the Inland Revenue enforced a UK tax levy upon the emoluments of one unfortunate expatriate who, prior to working abroad for a period that included a full tax year, sustained critical gunshot wounds while being robbed in West Africa.

Near death he was repatriated by ambulance plane; he spent several months in hospital, thankfully recovered and, not un-naturally, decided that he would not return to his overseas posting. His salary and all the other things that went to make up his substantial emoluments package during his six or seven months abroad were assessed for UK tax of over £10,000. And £10,000 was about as much cash as he had actually earned in the several months he was abroad and quite naturally he had spent a fair proportion of that. His employers, a major UK firm with an international reputation for both the excellence of their products and their personnel relationships, said that they would pay the £10,000 on his behalf. The Revenue said — very correctly — that if the employer did so they would regard that ex gratia payment as part of the poor injured man's emoluments and tax it too.

I have not made up this story; I was personally involved in helping to lessen the greater tax liabilities that there might have been.

Neither have I recounted the sorry tale here with the intention of implying any unpardonable inhumanity on the part of officers of the Inland Revenue; their duty is to enforce the law.

I have told you of it to underline the problems which can arise due to an early return to the UK; whether that return be simply unwise or unavoidable.

Remember that the reason for the return does not have to be as dramatic as that which I have recounted. Many expatriates do find that life abroad is beyond their ability to accept change; that is totally understandable. Differences in culture, climate and surrounding can play havoc with the best of intentions; missing friends and relatives back home is often the cause.

Other expatriates, although loving the life and the opportunities a job abroad can bring, suddenly find that they have to return early because of a failure in the contract which is not their fault. What ever the reason [and it is estimated that one in seven expatriates faces the problem] the tax imposts can be onerous since the Revenue will correctly contend that whilst having worked abroad for a while the expatriate has remained wholly resident and ordinarily resident within the UK for tax purposes if he did not work abroad for a period which included a full tax year.

Is there any relief available if such circumstances do arise?

The most minor relief will be the **personal allowance** given against UK income tax and the relief [now indexed] given to capital gains.

But the personal allowance will not greatly reduce a liability to tax on many overseas emolument packages. Currently a married man's personal allowance in the UK is £3,655; that does not lessen the tax imposition on £100,000 by a great deal!

Where else might the expatriate seek shelter?

Well, he might be able to claim that whilst abroad he was assessed for tax as a resident of the country in which he was working. There are more countries in the world who charge income tax than there are those who do not, remember.

Provided he has been working in such a country and that country has a **double tax treaty** with the United Kingdom then his income will not be subject to tax on the same emoluments in both countries. The Revenue will give him "credit" for the amount of tax he has paid in the foreign country so that their demand might not be as sizeable as it otherwise would.

The Revenue also have the power to afford **unilateral relief** to someone who has worked abroad for a while and paid tax to a country which does not subscribe to a double tax treaty with the UK. It is fair minded and understanding of the Revenue to accept that the greatest hardship could result if they clawed tax from an income that had already suffered tax in a country with whom no agreement had been concluded.

They proffered a measure of unilateral relief in the case of the expatriate who was ambushed in West Africa.

Those are two ways in which the UK tax liability might be lessened.

If you look at them closely you will discover that the areas of the world which do not charge tax are usually those in which many expatriates find it difficult to live; areas which are perhaps more affected by political strife. Or perhaps areas where medical facilities might not be "up to scratch" and which therefore are unable to provide long term treatment for serious illness or debility.

Such areas might also be those in which women do not find it easy to obtain employment. Psychological pressure might result in the wife returning home and thus making it harder for the husband to remain abroad alone.

Statistics also show that some thirty five per cent of all British expatriates work in these no tax areas. Therefore the chances of claiming relief under a double tax treaty or receiving unilateral relief are often low.

What else is available to relieve the burden?

Finance Act 1977

The Finance Act 1977 was introduced to provide measures of relief from UK tax on the world wide emoluments [not unearned income or capital gains] of those who went abroad to work but did not do so with the intention of doing so for a period which included a full tax year or who, as part of their employment, had to perform substantive duties within the UK as well as abroad.

When the legislation was enacted it was primarily intended to benefit those at "the sharp end" of British industry; those who, although resident for tax in the UK, spent the greater part of their working year selling British services and products by travelling to visit and arrange contracts with foreign buyers. Almost perchance what many now describe as **"short term expatriates"** were embraced by this legislation.

It is very much to their benefit that they were since many people set out to work abroad for a period which does not entitle them to be regarded as non-resident within the UK. Others, as I have explained, have their period abroad foreshortened for one reason or the other and might be eligible to receive relief under the 1977 legislation.

Originally the legislation contained relief for those who worked abroad for as little as a month in aggregate during a fiscal year; 25 per cent deduction from the UK tax liability on the emoluments was given.

Then the law was changed; that deduction was reduced to 12.5 per cent and then abolished altogether. **It is now a matter of "all or nowt"!**

The one remaining deduction under this legislation is the ultimate; if a short term expatriate follows the rules correctly he receives 100 per cent deduction from his tax liability on his world wide emoluments. IF he follows the rules correctly!

To have any chance of doing that he has to know what the rules are and that is where the difficulties start. You can compare the problems of anyone unused to the Finance Act 1977 rules with the plight of anyone who would be foolish enough to sit down and play mahjong with a crafty Hong Kong devotee of the game.

The very first thing that you must understand is that the Finance Act 1977 legislation applies only to those who although working abroad do so for a period which does not encapsulate a full tax year OR who, in working abroad for a period which does, breach the non-residence rules by, perhaps, performing substantive duties in the UK or spending too much time there.

Before we proceed any further let us stop and look at a couple of examples which might help set the scene.

Bill Bloggs leaves the UK on 30th September 1986 with the intention of working in Oman until 30th January 1988. Obviously he will not work abroad for a period that includes a full tax year. Thus in the entire period he works abroad he will remain resident for UK tax purposes. **His** *only hope of obtaining substantial relief from UK tax is the Finance Act 1977.*

Charlie Chick leaves the UK on 30th September 1986 with the intention of working in Oman until 30th January 1989. Since he can show every intention of working abroad for a period which does include a full tax year [1987-88] he can apply to be regarded as provisionally not resident and not ordinarily resident.

However, on 30th January 1988 Charlie finishes his contract abroad earlier than anticipated. It matters not at all why. Charlie's problem is that during the entire period that he was working abroad he remained resident and ordinarily resident for UK tax purposes exposing all his emoluments to a charge to UK tax. He did not work abroad for a period which includes a full tax year either.

***His** only hope of obtaining relief from UK tax [other than his personal allowance] is the 1977 Finance Act too.*

So you may see that both short term expatriates, like Bill, and an intending non-resident expatriate, like Charlie, have need of the help which the Finance Act 1977 might afford.

The Finance Act 1977 is a very important piece of UK fiscal legislation and can only be ignored at your peril.

Now to the complexities of that legislation; but before the explanation may I please ask that you consider each statement carefully and not to pass to the next stage before you feel that you understand what you are being told. You will have taken a great step forward if you can understand the situation. You might even become the only expatriate in your area that does!

Step 1

In order to qualify for the 100 per cent deduction an expatriate has to satisfy the Inland Revenue that he has been abroad **for a qualifying period of at least 365 days.** That means that if he is going abroad to work for only 100, 200 or even 300 days he will get no deduction. Although such a person might have had to pay tax in the country in which he was temporarily working. If so, and that country has a double tax treaty with the UK, then he might expect relief from UK tax under the terms of the treaty.

Step 2

The Finance Act 1977 defines a qualifying period as **a period of consecutive days which consists either of**

a] **days of absence from the UK**

or

b] **consists partly of such days and partly of intervening days in the period which is being considered for the 100 per cent deduction.**

For this purpose a day abroad is a day the **end** of which is spent abroad. Thus, if you leave the UK at 23.50 hrs you spend the day abroad; if you leave at 01.10 hrs you have to wait until midnight that day before you can claim to be abroad. Arrive in the UK at 23.50 hrs and you will be regarded as having been there all day.

Step 3
A qualifying period can look like this

Diagram 1

Day 1 leaves UK	→	remaining abroad for the entire time until	→	Day 366+ returns UK

or like this

Diagram 2

Abroad	UK	Abroad

The proviso being

a] **that there shall be at least 365 qualifying days in the period** and
b] **that if any of those qualifying days are spent in the UK there must not be more than 62 intervening days between absences abroad,** and
c] **the number of days in the period under consideration which are not days of absence from the UK must not exceed ⅙th of the total number of days in the relevant period.**

Subsequent periods in the UK followed by periods abroad are added to the initial qualifying period as they arise to form a single qualifying period.

Confused?!

Let me try to explain.

In **diagram 1** the minimum period of 365 days has been spent abroad.

The entire emoluments earned in the period abroad will receive the 100 per cent deduction. The "short term expatriate" to whom this diagram applies will have remained resident for UK tax on his emoluments but receive a deduction of 100 per cent against his liability.

In **diagram 2** some of the 365 days have been spent in the UK; all in one go. Provided they do not exceed 62 days [62 being roughly ⅙th of 365] once again the emoluments earned in the entire period will receive the 100 per cent deduction because the 62 days spent in the UK will be considered as having been spent abroad.

Now look at **diagram 3**

Diagram 3

A Abroad	B UK	C Abroad	D UK	E Abroad

Here, the days in the UK are in two distinct portions, separated by a period spent abroad. The legislation requires that

a] **the entire period ABCDE shall be at least 365 days long**

b] **the days spent in the UK shall not exceed 1/6th of the total of themselves plus the period either side of them. In other words, in the period ABC, B must be less than one sixth of the total of A+B+C.**

It will be a little easier to understand if we put some figures into the diagram.

Diagram 4

A Abroad 30	B UK 28	C Abroad 60	D UK 10	E Abroad 240	Total 368

Now let us apply the rules, the first of which is that **there must be more than 365 days;** we have 368 days so we are all right so far.

The next is that **the days spent in the UK must be less than 1/6th of the period "abroad-UK-abroad" of which they form a part.** The first section we need to look at then is ABC; we have to ask ourselves "is B greater than 1/6th of the whole A+B+C?"

A+B+C = 118 days; one sixth of 118 days is [to the nearest whole day] 20 days!

The section of the time abroad that we have looked at first has failed the test of what is commonly known as "the one sixth rule", because 28 days were spent in the UK during the period.

The remaining days do not add up to the necessary 365 days needed to qualify for the deduction and so the poor short term expatriate who works according to the example we have taken will receive no relief from UK tax on his overseas emoluments other than his normal personal allowance.

While we are at it, let us look at another example. And so as not to exercise our arithmetical abilities too much let us leave the figures as they were in diagram 4; to prevent boredom we shall just change the placing of the days spent in the UK.

Diagram 5

A Abroad 30	B UK 10	C Abroad 60	D UK 28	E Abroad 240	Total 368

The same 368 days so we know that the whole period meets the basic requirement that it should be at least 365 days long.

Next we have to take A+B+C and see whether B is more or less than one sixth of the total. 30+10+60 = 100 of which one sixth is [to the nearest whole day] 17. **The first period passes the test!** The days spent in the UK [for whatever purpose] do not exceed the limits. We are on our way!

The next period to look at is CDE; **I know that we are including the 60 days spent abroad [C] twice in our calculations but remember the requirement of the legislation? We need to calculate the days spent in the UK within the period as a fraction of the slices of work abroad either side of it.** CDE is 328 days in total; one sixth is 55 days [near enough] and total days spent in the UK [B and D] are less than one sixth of ABCDE.

The short term expatriate to whom this diagram refers will receive 100 per cent deduction from his UK tax liability on his UK emoluments.

And the only difference between the two diagrams is that we switched the periods spent in the UK. Can you imagine the frustration of a man who goes abroad to work on exactly the same day as his mate, spends *exactly* the same amount of time working abroad and on leave in the UK as his mate, and then discovers that he has to pay UK tax on his emoluments while his mate gets 100 per cent relief from UK tax on his earnings? Hang the frustration! Can you imagine the tax liability?

I think that it would be a good idea if I were to give you a couple of further examples and leave you to do the calculations. I shall tell you the correct answers later but please try not to cheat! It will really be a great help to you if you work them out for yourself by using the rules we have looked at so far.

Calculate please whether the two short term working British expatriates whose jobs abroad are covered by the following examples qualify at all for the 100 per cent deduction.

Be warned! One of the examples is sneaky; but if you really understand the regulations you will spot it.

Diagram 6

A	B	C	D	E	F	G	H	I
Abroad	UK	Abroad	UK	Abroad	UK	Abroad	UK	Abroad
78	13	85	18	99	15	57	13	172

Diagram 7

A	B	C	D	E	F	G	H	I	J	K
Abroad	UK	Abroad	UK	Abroad	UK	Abroad	UK	Abroad	UK	Abroad
100	35	69	10	16	4	77	7	14	3	166

Please do not cheat!

Diagram 6 is a pretty straight forward calculation and a satisfying result for the individual concerned. All the way through the employment he managed to arrange his visits to the UK so as to conform to the "one sixth" rule. The total number of days was in excess of 365 and thus he obtains the 100 per cent deduction from his emoluments.

Diagram 7 is the "sneaky" one! I can only hope that you did not give up the ghost when you discovered that in the period ABC there was a total of 204 days but that the individual had exceeded his permitted time in the UK by 3 days. If you threw into the waste-paper basket his chances of getting the 100 per cent deduction applied to at least part of his income, you were wrong! **You should have started again at C and re-calculated his position.** If you had then you would have found that the period CDEFGHIJK conforms to the regulations all along the line; there are 366 qualifying days [one over the minimum] and at no time did he offend the one sixth rule. His emoluments from C onward would have received the 100 per cent deduction. The emoluments for the two initial periods which failed the tests will be subjected to UK tax in the normal way.

Such examples are all very well. Days in and out of the UK can be manipulated to comply with or contravene the regulations. They can be made to prove a point or to point out some imagined expat's stupidity; we can all be clever when it doesn't really matter.

Rarely can real expatriates control their lives in this way; they are not able to determine their to-ing and fro-ing with such precise, clinical accuracy. An urgent business meeting, the sudden, unexpected need to be with the UK-based family in an emergency; anything can happen when it is least expected or desirable.

The short term expatriate should have a working knowledge of the rules before he goes abroad and do his level best to live within them; perhaps by meeting his family in a European city rather than return to the UK for a special anniversary. What tends to be far more disturbing is for the long term expatriate, who had every intention of working abroad for a long enough period to become non-resident, to find himself — some 400 days, say, into his job abroad — having to return to the UK permanently and unscheduled. If, during his early period abroad he had paid several visits to the UK, to consult with his employers, to attend a funeral, to get medical treatment or what ever, he might well find that his plans are not only thwarted as far as becoming non-resident but also that he does not comply with the requirements of the Finance Act 1977. The entire emoluments earned whilst he was working abroad will be subjected to UK tax; as will any capital gains or unearned income. He will have remained resident in the UK and will pay the penalty.

The penalty being a UK tax liability upon the whole of his emoluments; not nice!

The "one sixth rule" causes more expatriates more headaches than practically any thing else. Largely because they do not understand the regulations or the ramifications of their abuse.

Some times the headaches are real enough; many times the pain is "psychological".

Some expats have no reason, what so ever, to feel the dread of the onset of any fiscal illness brought about by not following the law contained in the Finance Act 1977.

If you are already a working expatriate it might be very useful if you were to determine now whether you have any need to worry about the "one sixth rule".

If you answer "NO" to any of the following questions then you must remain continuously wary of the 1977 legislation.

a] have you worked abroad in full time employment for a period which encompasses a full UK fiscal year?

b] if you have worked abroad for a period which encompasses a full fiscal year can you be certain that any duties which you have performed in the UK will be regarded as "merely incidental" to your overseas employment?

Directors of overseas companies who have performed duties of their office within UK need not concern themselves with the meaning of "merely incidental" duties. They can only hope, when the UK Revenue finds out about their activities, that their visits to the UK will accord with the requirements of the one sixth rule.

Before I issue one final word of warning about this somewhat tiresome legislation we should note that the rules can work in a short term expatriate's favour by shielding him from foreign taxes. Under the agreements hammered out in double tax treaties that it has with most countries the UK reserves the right to tax its residents. If, for example, a short term expatriate went to work in America for a twelve month period [beginning other than on 1st January, the start of the USA tax year] for a UK or foreign employer who had no permanent place of business there then he would not become liable to US tax. If he followed the one sixth rule he would be "forgiven" his tax liability by the UK Revenue. Under the UK-USA treaty he would fall liable to UK tax because he has remained a resident there [not having worked abroad for a period which included a tax year] but could claim 100 per cent deduction. Only on his emoluments, remember!

The final word of warning is in two parts.

Firstly, do not be deceived, by anyone, into the mistake of thinking that if you transgress the one sixth rule only you will ever know. The chances are very high that under examination by the Revenue the flaw will be reported. And even higher are the chances that it will be *you* who tells! When push turns to shove very few people have it in their hearts to "tell fibs' to the Revenue; remember that it is not the aim of the Revenue to wring confessions out of anyone but it is the duty of any UK tax resident to give the Revenue the correct facts in order that it might be established whether or not a liability to UK tax exists.

Conversely many working expatriates who realise that they have trangressed the rules lose heart entirely; they throw in the towel; they too readily assume that "the game is up" and return home to the UK to face the music when a few more weeks abroad, even on holiday, can mitigate their UK tax liability or eradicate it altogether. If in any doubt about your situation consult an expert before you return to the UK.

The second part of the warning is that there is a great deal of misleading information available to you on the practical application of the "one sixth rule". If anyone [including a very well known High Street Bank via their brochures on the subject] tells you that all you have to do to ensure compliance with the Finance Act 1977 is to make sure that you spend less than one sixth of your overseas contract within the UK then ignore them. Especially if, as does the brochure of this famous bank, they tell you that provided you spend no more than 62 days in the UK out of the minimum period of 365 qualifying days you will be "all right". Ignore them.

I cannot stress enough my opinion that working expatriates need professional advice in all matters, but it is particularly important to find someone whose prime objective is not simply "flogging" you investments or life policies; someone who understands the tax implications of working abroad as well as investment schemes.

Whenever you are in any doubt, what so ever, about your position vis a vis the UK Revenue and the laws which they administer so well, obtain the professional opinion of someone well versed in the complexities of the Finance Act 1977 or the laws pertaining to UK tax residence as they apply to working expatriates.

The expert will know which way the cat can jump and will probably tell you that there is little or no point in seeing how far it will jump by going back to the UK un-necessarily and, from close quarters, shouting "boo" in its ear!

To avoid un-necessary panics it is always as well to keep a record of your days in and out of the UK as your term abroad progresses.

Even if you can foresee no requirement to "hide" under the "one sixth rule", even if it is your firm intention to become not resident and not ordinarily resident, being prepared for problems never hurts. Try keeping a chart, much like the examples I have given you, and at the end of each visit to the UK do the calculations as I have shown you how. Once you have worked abroad in full time and continuous employment for a period which includes at least one full tax year you have my permission to stop worrying about the effects of the Finance Act 1977; the regulations will no longer apply to you provided, of course, that the only duties which you have performed in the UK can be considered "merely incidental" to your overseas employment.

Do, please, remember that to have any chance of becoming not resident and not ordinarily resident an expatriate must work abroad for at least one full tax year. Timing, in this respect can be crucial.

Anyone who leaves the UK to work full time abroad on 4th April 1987 and returns permanently on 7th April 1988 will be able to claim that he was non-resident. And he has only been away for little over a year; in which time he can spend holidays in the UK.

An expatriate who leaves the UK to work abroad on 7th April 1987 will have to wait right-round until 6th April 1989 before he can stop worrying about the one sixth rule.

As the song says "what a difference a day makes".

UK source income

I have already told you, right at the start of this chapter that one of the objectives of the Inland Revenue is to tax any income arising within the UK no matter to whom that income belongs.

In the case of an expatriate who is not resident for a whole tax year such UK source income will be the only money upon which UK tax will be assessed.

Emoluments paid in the UK but earned wholly overseas by a non-resident working British expatriate are not regarded as UK source income.

Many expatriates find that it is convenient to have part of their overseas emoluments paid in the UK. Perhaps because they want to have sterling available to meet outstanding liabilities in the UK or, just as likely, because the country in which they are working imposes stringent exchange control regulations on the repatriation of earnings. Whatever the reason, whether paid wholly in sterling and paid wholly in the UK, or paid partly abroad and partly in a foreign currency, **the overseas emoluments of a working British expatriate are free of UK tax provided that he is non-resident within the UK.**

However, most other incomes which arise in the UK suffer UK tax; normally at source. The Revenue sometimes finds it more efficient to waive a liability to tax on certain UK source incomes which are paid to the recipient gross. State pension payments, for example, have no clawback of tax in the UK when paid to a non-resident. But by and large all other incomes arising in the UK are regarded as being fair game for the Revenue's requirements. **In particular rents received from the leasing of property in the UK are always subjected to UK tax.**

I shall deal in greater depth with that subject in the part of the book dealing with the letting of UK property. Suffice it here to say that many thousands of working British expatriates overlook, by accident or design, their continuing liability to UK tax on this type of income from rented property.

They do so at great risk to their continuing financial well-being since, without a doubt, the Revenue will discover the "oversight" and, quite rightly, require to be paid the tax that has been due; maybe for several years and, just as likely, subject to penalties for late payment.

The other forms of income that are most likely to arise in the UK are from UK based investment, from interest bearing bank or building society accounts in the UK or from pensions paid from the UK.

UK bank and building society interest

For many years UK bank interest, although subject to a liability to income tax if the account holder is a UK tax resident, has not been subject to the "witholding tax" if the account is held by someone not ordinarily resident within the UK.

In April 1986 the same benefit was bestowed [belatedly] on the interest derived from a building society account provided that you are not ordinarily resident within the UK. Expatriates who are designated not resident for a tax year **but who remain ordinarily resident within the UK** will still have to suffer UK tax deductions from interest earned from UK banks or building societies.

If you insist on keeping your deposit accounts in the United Kingdom then you will need to sign a declaration to the bank concerned that you are not ordinarily resident within the UK and will tell them of any changes in your tax status that might affect their paying you the interest gross.

Other interest you receive may, by concession, be paid to you without deduction of tax provided that you are treated as non-resident for the whole of the tax year in which the interest is received.

This concession does not apply where

a] the interest is paid to an agent of yours in the UK

or

b] the UK tax can be set off against a claim to relief for partial UK personal allowance.

Having mentioned that subject it would be as well to deal with it now although few working British expatriates should consider the possibilities.

Partial personal allowance

In general no personal allowances are available in the UK to those who are non-resident there. However, it is possible for a working British expatriate to claim that, although he is non-resident, he has certain income arising in the UK against which he seeks personal allowance relief.

The Revenue will consider his claim and will, normally, be happy to acceed to his requirements provided he is prepared to divulge his overseas income. UK source income is then calculated as a percentage of the total worldwide income and the appropriate percentage of personal allowance is given.

This may be particularly advantageous to an expatriate who is in receipt of a pension from a previous UK employer; perhaps from one of HM Forces.

UK pensions

A pension payable by a previous employer continues to be taxable in the hands of a non-resident if it is payable from a UK source. With the exception of the State pension and very specific schemes [like the Central African Pension Fund] all UK pensions are taxable at source and little can be done to minimise the UK liability other than to claim relief under a double tax treaty or to apply for partial personal allowance in the UK.

It is rare that in other than these circumstances claiming partial personal allowance is in the interest of the expatriate; very rare indeed; unless his UK income is a substantial part of his world-wide income.

Then it might be worth while but remember the calculation of the figures takes time, the preparation of the claim takes time and professionl time is expensive.

Also remember that you also need to reveal the extent of other income arising around the world. Not always advisable! Even if, as someone not resident within the UK, you will not suffer UK income tax upon the foreign emoluments.

UK investment income

Working expatriates who are non-resident within the United Kingdom still may have a liability to pay UK income tax on UK source investment income.

Normally anyone resident in the UK for tax purposes who gets a dividend from his investments in a UK resident company is taxable on the gross equivalent of that dividend. If he receives £213 he has had, in effect, cash of £300 taxed at 29%. If his marginal rate of tax were 55% he has a further liability to tax on the difference between the tax with which he has been "credited" and his actual rate of tax. In this example he would pay a further £78 in tax, ie £300 @ [55-29]%.

Those of you who are not resident receive no tax credits unless you are working in a country with whom the UK has a double tax treaty [when a miserable 50% of the tax credit is allowed] or when, rarely, it might pay to claim partial personal allowance.

Double tax treaties

Basically the idea of any double tax treaty is a concession on the part of both countries who are signatories to the agreement not to charge tax twice on the same income or capital.

Detailed information on any one of the scores of double tax treaties which the UK has with other countries can be obtained by writing to **The Secretary, The Board of the Inland Revenue, Somerset House, London WC2 1LB.**

Never dismiss as too complex the details of any treaty between the country in which you are living and the UK. It is sometimes possible [often, would be a better word I suppose] to be regarded as resident for tax in two or more countries of the world at the same time. Residents are, normally, charged tax in any country. The complications arise when, if DTA's exist, it has to be determined which country is going to do the charging to tax of the income or capital appreciation. The complexities are brought about by the fact that the countries concerned might have different "tests" which a person might undergo for it to be decided whether or not he is resident for tax purposes.

The "tests" are pretty standard.

If a person is living in two or more places for part of a year [for example he may work for a British firm abroad and spend part of the year in Spain, another part in Italy and yet another part in the UK] then obviously three tax regimes will want to see if they have a right to tax him. The tests are designed to see who has the right and what will be investigated [and the order in which the matters will be investigated] is

i] where has he his permanent home or

ii] where has he his centre of vital interest or
iii] where is his habitual abode or
iv] of which country is he a national.

In the example I have cited the chances are that if the man is working for a UK firm, is a national of Britain, has a home in Britain and spends as much time in Britain as he does anywhere else then the UK is the place that will assess whether there is a tax liability for him to answer. If such a man is flitting between these three countries then it is highly likely that he will be regarded as resident and ordinarily resident in the UK and all he will get is a personal allowance.

A relief, rather than an allowance, which it is practically always advantageous to ensure that you receive — provided that you are entitled to it — is Mortgage Interest Relief At Source [MIRAS].

MIRAS

Mortgage Interest Relief At Source was introduced in 1983, allowing mortgate interest paid to a qualifying lender to be paid net of the standard rate of income tax [now 29%]. Practically all UK bank, building society and life company mortgages will qualify for MIRAS.

At first sight [and indeed on the first announcements of the Revenue] it appeared that the legislation precluded working expatriates from the new system but happily that is not the case.

The property must be the only or main residence of the borrower or the main residence of a dependent relative, his wife or, indeed, a separated or former wife. For MIRAS to be applicable the mortgage must not exceed £30,000.

A working British expatriate, who leaves his family back home in the UK will receive MIRAS for the entire length of his period abroad provided that his wife [or separated or former wife] occupies the house as her main residence for a minimum of three months in four years.

A working British expatriate whose wife and dependent children live with him abroad and who leaves his home occupied by tenants may continue to receive MIRAS for four years starting from the date of his going to work abroad. If he [he would have to be very careful or very stupid if he did it in one tax year!] or his wife occupies the house for a minimum of three months within the four year period then a further four year period becomes effective.

The proviso is that he must have regarded the property as his principal private residence before he left the UK.

If, during a period of leave, he buys a property he will only be entitled to MIRAS provided that he occupies the house as his only [or main] residence for a minimum of three months before he returns abroad. If he did he would, as you will have learned from comment at the start of this chapter, be close to breaching the 90 day rule if in previous [or following] years he spent several weeks in the UK.

Since, however, the MIRAS regulations recognise occupation by a wife as being

enough to establish the house as the main residence the MIRAS requirements would be adhered to were his wife to remain in the UK for that period.

MIRAS is even available to expatriates who let their homes to tenants where it is more to his benefit to receive relief on interest this way rather than relief against rental income; that relief is discussed in the UK Home Chapter.

The following chart might help establish whether or not you are entitled to MIRAS. If you are and if you are currently not claiming it then you should write immediately to the building society, bank or life company from whom you obtained the mortgage and explain your circumstances.

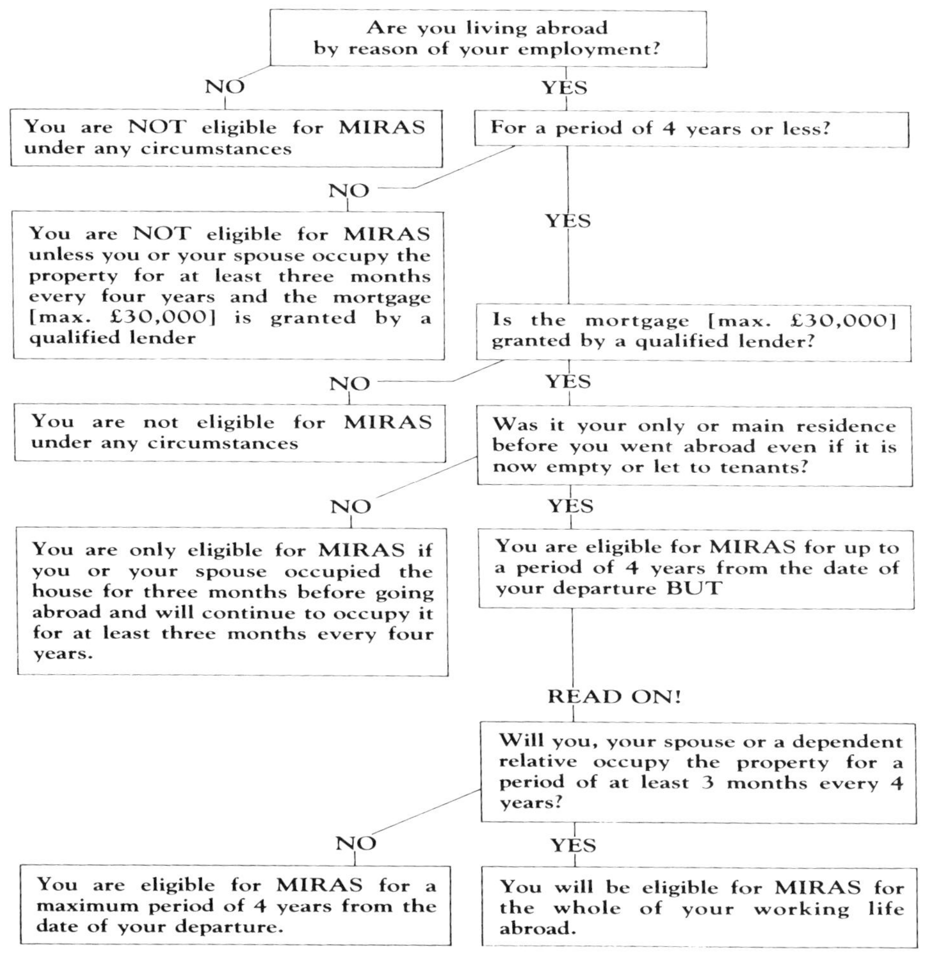

Are you living abroad by reason of your employment?
NO
You are NOT eligible for MIRAS under any circumstances
YES
For a period of 4 years or less?
NO
You are NOT eligible for MIRAS unless you or your spouse occupy the property for at least three months every four years and the mortgage [max. £30,000] is granted by a qualified lender
YES
Is the mortgage [max. £30,000] granted by a qualified lender?
NO
You are not eligible for MIRAS under any circumstances
YES
Was it your only or main residence before you went abroad even if it is now empty or let to tenants?
NO
You are only eligible for MIRAS if you or your spouse occupied the house for three months before going abroad and will continue to occupy it for at least three months every four years.
YES
You are eligible for MIRAS for up to a period of 4 years from the date of your departure BUT
READ ON!
Will you, your spouse or a dependent relative occupy the property for a period of at least 3 months every 4 years?
NO
You are eligible for MIRAS for a maximum period of 4 years from the date of your departure.
YES
You will be eligible for MIRAS for the whole of your working life abroad.

Termination payments

It is a sad fact of modern commercial life that no-one's job is secure. However caring and prestigious the employer, however long you might have worked for him, you could find that you are recalled back to the UK to be told that as a result of a planned merger, failure of a contract or two, economic recession or what ever package of disaster the news comes wrapped in, you are no longer required.

The recompense for the news will be determined by whether your contract of employment is with a British company or a foreign employer. The rules relating to compensation by foreign employers differ so much from country to country that the only advice in these circumstances is that if you are not satisfied with the amount of cash you are being offered you ought consult an international lawyer skilled in the crafty art of arbitration.

If your employer is British then you have certain rights and, with the help of a British lawyer, you ought ensure that you receive the benefits to which you are entitled.

If your contract is terminated while you are a UK resident then you may well be taxable on any compensation or ex gratia payment you receive. As of 4th June 1986 the rules for charging these sums to UK tax have been amended. Sums up to £25,000 are free of UK tax, between £25,000 and £75,000 the tax liability is chargeable at half the applicable rates. The payment is regarded as the top slice of income. Between £75,000 and £100,000 the charge is three quarters of the applicable rates and anything over £100,000 is taxed in full.

If compensation is given whilst you are still wholly not resident and not ordinarily resident then the sum, whatever the size, is free of UK tax. The date of termination of the contract is important since that will determine whether, if you receive the payment once you have returned to resume residence, you will receive the payment free of UK tax or whether only the first £25,000 will be exempt and the rest made to suffer tax.

I have tried to sum up the basic rules which will determine your liabilities to UK tax on world wide income in the following "flow chart". It is not comprehensive and I have included it only to encourage you to look at it and then, having followed the path dictated by your circumstances, to look again at the sections of this chapter which cover the situations in far greater detail than any flow chart can ever hope to do.

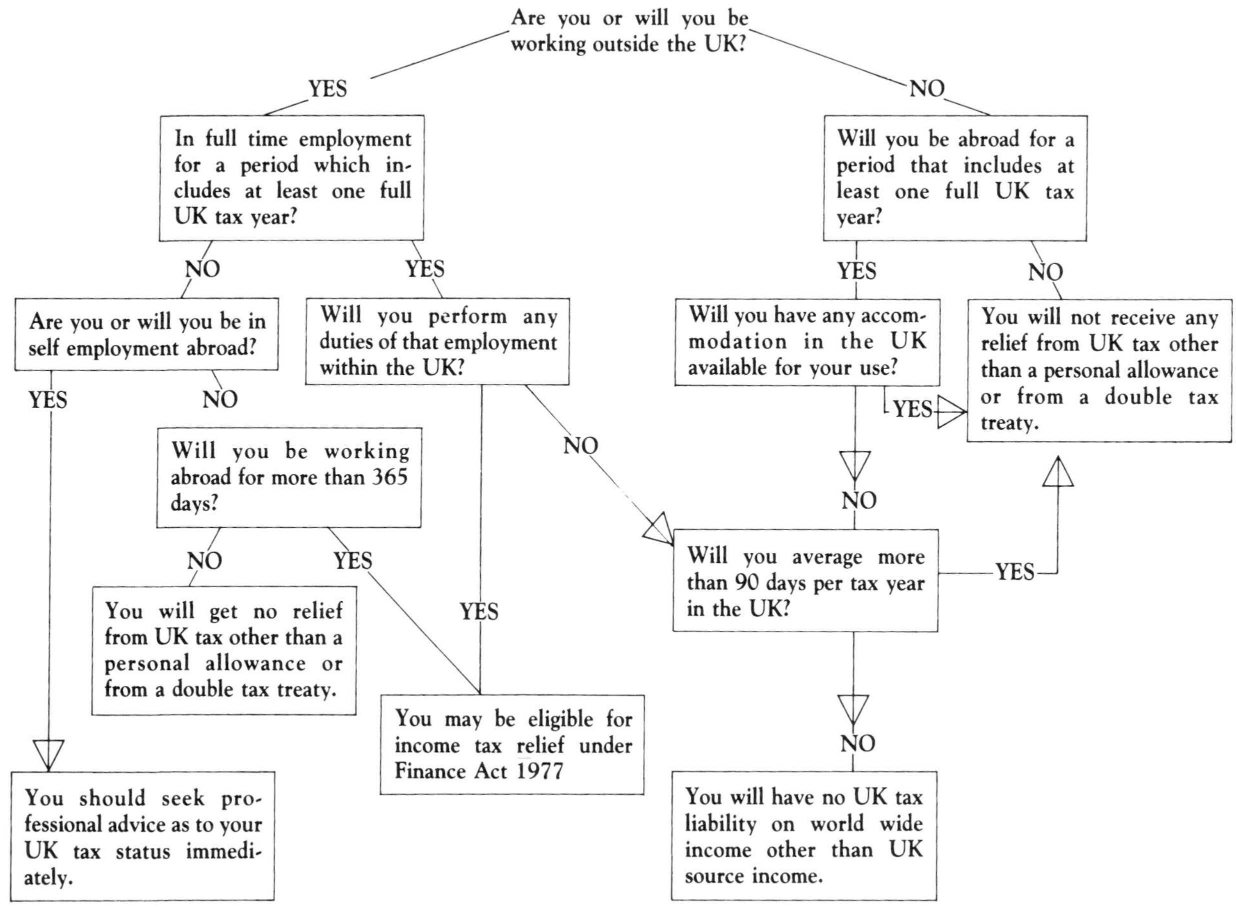
Are you or will you be working outside the UK?
YES
NO
In full time employment for a period which includes at least one full UK tax year?
Will you be abroad for a period that includes at least one full UK tax year?
NO
YES
YES
NO
Are you or will you be in self employment abroad?
Will you perform any duties of that employment within the UK?
Will you have any accommodation in the UK available for your use?
You will not receive any relief from UK tax other than a personal allowance or from a double tax treaty.
YES
NO
YES
NO
Will you be working abroad for more than 365 days?
NO
NO
NO
YES
YES
Will you average more than 90 days per tax year in the UK?
YES
You will get no relief from UK tax other than a personal allowance or from a double tax treaty.
You may be eligible for income tax relief under Finance Act 1977
NO
You should seek professional advice as to your UK tax status immediately.
You will have no UK tax liability on world wide income other than UK source income.

CAPITAL GAINS TAX

An individual's liability to UK capital gains tax also turns on his residence or ordinary residence there.

CGT [@ 30%] is assessed on any chargeable gain on the disposal of an asset, no matter where in the world that asset might be situated during a year in which the individual is either resident or ordinarily resident. Therefore to be free of CGT a working expatriate must be both not resident and not ordinarily resident for the whole year in which the disposal is made.

I have said it before, I shall say it again, **the short term expatriate who seeks relief from UK income tax under the "one sixth rule" has no protection from CGT.**

Those who go out on a longer term with the intention of becoming wholly not resident and not ordinarily resident still have to watch when they make disposals if CGT is to be avoided. Let us look at the tax treatment in the year of departure.

Technically anyone who makes a profitable disposal of an asset in a year [tax year!] during any part of which he was regarded as resident within the UK will incur a liability to CGT. But by concession the Revenue will afford relief during the year of departure on any disposals made after the date of departure.

That means, in essence, that a long term expatriate has two bites of the cherry. He may dispose of assets prior to his departure and take advantage of the annual exemption given to UK residents [£6,300 for 1986/87] and, once he is abroad, dispose of other assets in the year of his departure.

Much the same applies in his year of return where an individual is to be regarded as resident from the date of his arrival in the UK.

Under the law he should be taxed on any disposal made **during the year of his return** whether he makes the disposal before or after his return.

However, and again by Revenue concession, **where an individual has been not resident and not ordinarily resident during the 36 months preceding his return he is taxed only on gains arising after the date of his arrival.** Again he can use the annual CGT allowance [applicable to his year of return] once he has returned.

If the assignment abroad was less than 36 months in duration then the concession in the year of return does not apply.

To escape a liability to UK CGT any expatriate who has been regarded as not resident and not ordinarily resident for less than 36 months should take care to reassess his situation prior to the start of the tax year of his return; long term planning is required. Since we are talking of trying to decide so long in advance what assets to sell, "long term guessing" might be a more appropriate phrase!

Until recently the Revenue held that the normal exemption for CGT on disposals of assets between spouses did not apply where one spouse was not resident and the other resident.

In working expatriate situations such circumstances often arose; the husband worked abroad, the wife stayed in the UK. He was non-resident, she was resident.

The Revenue's practice was to insist that in such circumstances a husband and wife could not — in their opinion anyway — be "living together". The Revenue treated the couple as though they had become legally separated.

In a celebrated case *[Gubay v Kington]* the Revenue's understanding of the law was upset. The Law Lords ruled that a married couple each having a different residential status should still be regarded as "living together" for the purpose of CGT legislation.

Therefore it is possible that a resident spouse might make CGT free disposals to the non-resident spouse; the spouse abroad can then dispose of them free of CGT and hand back the cash. That is the theory, anyway. If you wish to consider such a move do not wander into such a complex area unadvised. As I said in the preface there are areas of tax mitigation which ought be marked "Here be dragons"; **this is decidedly one of them!**

The CGT implications of selling a UK dwelling are explored in the chapter on the UK home.

Part time employees

Throughout this chapter [and indeed I shall continue throughout the book] I have pointed out that I am, by and large, talking to British expatriates who are in full time employment abroad.

In the course of my working life I have been privileged to travel widely; thus far I have "clocked up" 140 countries of the world and well over a couple of million air-miles. I have lectured in most of those countries to members of the working British expatriate community. In each of the four well-rounded corners of the world I have also been lectured **at** by expatriates who reckon, quite wrongly, that so close are they to staying within the regulations the Revenue will forgive their "indiscretions".

Particularly vocal on this point have been expatriates who, whilst working abroad — perhaps for years at a time — are not in full time employment. They are either in part time employment or are self employed.

A considerable number of women expatriates, perhaps out of choice but more likely by reason of employment strictures placed upon them by the overseas country, work part time abroad.

They might be experienced teachers who find that the best they can do is work only a few hours a day. They might be dental nurses who have secured part time employment in a surgery abroad; they might even be employed part time by the husband's employer.

The wages/salary earned in such part time employment are only free of UK tax if

a] **by having no available accommodation in the UK and by restricting visits to less than 90 days on average per fiscal year the woman establishes herself as not resident and not ordinarily resident within the UK** OR b] **having accommodation available for her use during visits to the UK the woman has already suffered tax on her earnings in a country with whom the UK has a double tax treaty.**

Once again let me hasten to say that the gender of the part time worker does not determine this treatment. Women and men are treated equally in this regard. It just happens that more women work abroad in part time employment than do men.

Some expatriates expose themselves to a considerable amount of unnecessary worry on the point of what constitutes "part time employment", when, in reality, they are in full time employment overseas. A dental nurse, for example, may work only between 0800hrs and 1300hrs; part time? Not necessarily; the dentist might only open his surgery between those hours and thus she will be in full time employment.

Self employed

Many expatriates — both men and women — although working long and hard in an overseas territory, cannot claim to be in full time employment abroad. Sometimes their personal preferences, often the inhibitions of their profession [and now-a-days the crass ignorance of many firms] dictate that they should be self employed. Their overseas earnings are garnered by way of professional fees or under consultancy agreements.

The exemptions which I have dwelt on at some length as applying to those in full time employment abroad DO NOT APPLY TO THOSE WHO ARE SELF EMPLOYED.

Any expatriate who is self employed [dentists, doctors, musicians, journalists and the like] and working for fees or under a consultancy agreement should immediately seek professional advice on his UK tax liabilities if he has not already done so.

So too should anyone working on the UK sector of the continental shelf; members of HM Forces, British Government employees [such as members of the Diplomatic Service] and aircrew and seafarers [if their duties require them to call at airports or ports on the UK mainland].

Special rules apply to such people and individual professional advice on their affairs is of paramount importance.

Just as it is for anyone working abroad who has world wide assets in excess of £71,000.

INHERITANCE TAX

The UK Finance Act 1986 contained the obituary of capital transfer tax and announced the birth of inheritance tax. To all intent and purpose inheritance tax first saw the light of day in 1894 when, at eight pence in the pound and feared by all the landed gentry, it was introduced as Death Duty. As of 18th March 1986 tax upon life time transfers of assets is, by and large, abolished.

Now only transfers of assets which take place at death or within 7 years prior to death are liable for inheritance tax; the "inter vivos" transfers are taxed on a sliding scale.

Years between gift and death	Percentage of full charge at death rates
0-3	100%
3-4	80%
4-5	60%
5-6	40%
6-7	20%

The rates of inheritance tax upon death are as follows: they too, as you can see, are on a sliding scale.

£ chargeable band	% rate	£ total
1- 71,000	0	NIL
71,001- 95,000	30	7,200
95,001-129,000	35	19,100
129,001-164,000	40	33,100
164,001-206,000	45	52,000
206,001-257,000	50	77,500
257,001-317,000	55	110,500
over 317,000	60	

Certain exemptions which existed under capital transfer tax [such as transfers to a spouse] remain available under the new inheritance tax legislation.

The fact that a working expatriate is wholly non-resident within the UK does not lessen his liability to inheritance tax. Anyone domiciled or deemed to be domiciled within England, Northern Ireland, Scotland or Wales remains liable to inheritance tax just as he did under the capital transfer tax rules.

I promised that I should explore **domicile;** it will be a brief exploration!

You might already have noticed a whiff of the complexities involved when, just two paragraphs above, I was specific about your being domiciled or regarded as being domiciled in specific countries of Britain.

The concept of domicile is covered by far more complex rules, practices and legislative minefields than is tax residence. And the result is that it would need a tome many many times as thick as this book even to begin to scratch the surface of the subject.

I can therefore simply ask you to accept that if you were born in England, Northern Ireland, Scotland or Wales of parents born there or if, even though born abroad of parents born within Britain, you regard one of the countries of Britain as "home" then the 99.9% certainty is that you are domiciled within Britain.

If, whilst abroad, you have had children [albeit they were born abroad] the chances are just as great that they too are domiciled within Britain. Even though they may never yet have been to that part of Her Majesty's realm. Children are born with a tummy button and a domicile; just as they inherit a tendency to red hair, freckles, dimples or snub-noses from their parents they inevitably inherit the father's domicile too.

Please do not confuse domicile with nationality. It can very often happen that a person can be domiciled, out of choice, in one country whilst being a national of another.

Under internationally recognised rules you cannot change this domicile of origin. You may disguise it by adopting a domicile of choice or, in the case of some married women one of dependency but you cannot ever change your domicile of origin. No-one should ever attempt or even contemplate adopting another domicile without the expert help of a lawyer.

Just as with red hair or freckles, make up can be applied to hide domicile of origin; but it has to be applied carefully and professionally otherwise it has a tendency to wear off at a most inconvenient time. So if you are thinking of going to live permanently in a country other than the UK and in doing so intend that you should avoid inheritance tax **consult a lawyer.**

Most working British expatriates do not want to live anywhere else but the UK from the end of their working lives to the end of their lives. The majority of them will, therefore, remain boldly and proudly domiciled within Britain and be subject to inheritance tax at death. Some — may be all — will be subject to more inheritance tax than they ought unless they **consult a lawyer.**

Even if [and I suppose I ought really say IF!] you are wise enough to have a valid will, and even IF you are amongst the relatively few expatriates who altered their wills to take account of the introduction of capital transfer tax in 1974, you really ought start again; and that means that you should **consult a lawyer.**

Please do not think that you can incorporate everything that you need to incorporate in one of those awful "DIY" will forms of which so many expatriates are fond. Not only are most such wills not worth the paper they are written on; they are not worth the hassle that they create for dependants once you are beyond caring about where you were domiciled.

Personal counselling on tax matters

I did not even consider incorporating a "check list" which the average expatriate might try to follow in an attempt to establish a proper relationship between himself and the Inland Revenue.

In the whole wide world there is no such being as "the average expatriate" and the thought of many expatriates trying to establish a proper relationship between themselves and the Inland Revenue is something which, like mass suicide, I hesitate to contemplate.

To those few expatriates qualified to help themselves in this respect such a list

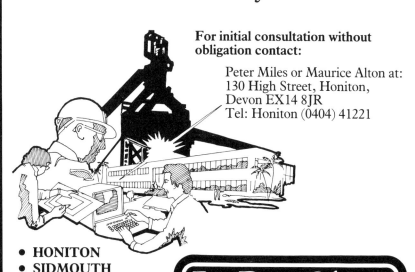

WORKING ABROAD?
Reader Enquiry Service

To find out more about the services of any advertiser in this edition of "Working Abroad?" simply complete this card and send it to the address shown overleaf. Your details will then be forwarded to the advertisers you choose.

- ☐ Aurigny Air Services
- ☐ Barclay Unicorn International
- ☐ Commercial Bank of Wales
- ☐ ERC — International Selection
- ☐ Fidelity International
- ☐ Gabbitas-Thring
- ☐ Hill Samuel & Co [Jersey] Ltd
- ☐ Jardine Fleming Investment
- ☐ MediCare
- ☐ NatWest Special Reserve
- ☐ Save & Prosper Group
- ☐ Shannon Kneale [Accountants]
- ☐ Tyndall Fund Managers
- ☐ Wingspan Travellers Club
- ☐ Banner Overseas Financial Services
- ☐ Britannia International Management
- ☐ Dunning & Co [Solicitors]
- ☐ Errolgrange Insurance Group
- ☐ Freemans International
- ☐ Guernsey Tourist Board
- ☐ LLoyds Bank Finance [Jersey] Ltd
- ☐ Midland Bank Trust Corporation
- ☐ Robeco
- ☐ School Fees Insurance Agency
- ☐ Trustee Savings Bank
- ☐ Unilife Assurance
- ☐ York House Financial Services

If you have any other areas of interest simply indicate them by ticking the appropriate box below. Your interest will be indicated to any future advertiser in EXPATXTRA! who offers services in these areas. If you use this facility you could receive a great deal of mail.

- ☐ Banking [Off-shore]
- ☐ Building Society Accounts
- ☐ Gift services
- ☐ Investment advice
- ☐ Investment Funds [off-shore]
- ☐ Life assurance
- ☐ Medical insurance
- ☐ Mediterranean Properties
- ☐ Pension plans
- ☐ School fees
- ☐ Tax counselling
- ☐ Travel
- ☐ UK car hire
- ☐ UK investment property

BLOCK CAPITALS PLEASE

NAME ....

ADDRESS ....

....

....

WORKING ABROAD?
Reader Enquiry Service

To find out more about the services of any advertiser in this edition of "Working Abroad?" simply complete this card and send it to the address shown overleaf. Your details will then be forwarded to the advertisers you choose.

- ☐ Aurigny Air Services
- ☐ Barclay Unicorn International
- ☐ Commercial Bank of Wales
- ☐ ERC — International Selection
- ☐ Fidelity International
- ☐ Gabbitas-Thring
- ☐ Hill Samuel & Co [Jersey] Ltd
- ☐ Jardine Fleming Investment
- ☐ MediCare
- ☐ NatWest Special Reserve
- ☐ Save & Prosper Group
- ☐ Shannon Kneale [Accountants]
- ☐ Tyndall Fund Managers
- ☐ Wingspan Travellers Club
- ☐ Banner Overseas Financial Services
- ☐ Britannia International Management
- ☐ Dunning & Co [Solicitors]
- ☐ Errolgrange Insurance Group
- ☐ Freemans International
- ☐ Guernsey Tourist Board
- ☐ LLoyds Bank Finance [Jersey] Ltd
- ☐ Midland Bank Trust Corporation
- ☐ Robeco
- ☐ School Fees Insurance Agency
- ☐ Trustee Savings Bank
- ☐ Unilife Assurance
- ☐ York House Financial Services

If you have any other areas of interest simply indicate them by ticking the appropriate box below. Your interest will be indicated to any future advertiser in EXPATXTRA! who offers services in these areas. If you use this facility you could receive a great deal of mail.

- ☐ Banking [Off-shore]
- ☐ Building Society Accounts
- ☐ Gift services
- ☐ Investment advice
- ☐ Investment Funds [off-shore]
- ☐ Life assurance
- ☐ Medical insurance
- ☐ Mediterranean Properties
- ☐ Pension plans
- ☐ School fees
- ☐ Tax counselling
- ☐ Travel
- ☐ UK car hire
- ☐ UK investment property

BLOCK CAPITALS PLEASE

NAME ....

ADDRESS ....

....

....

AIRMAIL

Affix
postage
here

READER SERVICES
PO BOX 300
JERSEY
CHANNEL ISLANDS

AIRMAIL

Affix
postage
here

READER SERVICES
PO BOX 300
JERSEY
CHANNEL ISLANDS

would have been worthless; to the thousands of expatriates totally unqualified to help themselves the list would have been worse than worthless.

This book, if it has any part to play in your fiscal and financial affairs, can do no more than can a book on family medicine for example. It can point out where aches and pains are likely to occur, possible reasons for blemishes that suddenly erupt and that some symptoms are relatively harmless while others, especially when they all appear at the same time, might indicate an ailment that warrants immediate professional advice. I am not offering a paliative; I am suggesting that you should always have professional counsellors to hand.

One-off financial advice is about as useless as one-off birth control; little mistakes which grow bigger by the hour are likely to result.

It constantly amazes me that whereas hundreds of thousands of working expatriates swallow capsules to ward off maleria or bare their arms [not to mention their bottoms] for injections of vaccine to prevent yellow fever, few and far between are those who bare anything to a trained fiscal or financial adviser until or unless the monetary sickness is reaching the terminal stage. So I am not going to add to the possibilities of your trying to go it alone when you simply cannot do so.

However you have got hold of this book; whether you have paid for it, been given it or borrowed it I hope that you will follow this one piece of advice if you follow no other that is contained within its covers.

Unless you are yourself professionally qualified to help yourself in matters financial turn to a profesional for help; attempt no DIY wills, do not treat with the Revenue yourself, consult bankers about banking, investment advisers about investments, qualified insurance brokers about insurance and, above all, tax consultants about tax.

Such consultants come in varying guises; accountants, of course, lawyers and specialists who have made in depth studies of the tax implications of working abroad. Banks, investment managers, stockbrokers, commodity brokers, insurance brokers and others may all have on their staff specialists in the tax field; people who can combine financial advice with guidance on the fiscal implications of saving, investment and life policies. In the section dealing specifically with banking, insurance and investment I shall comment on how to go about choosing an adviser in those fields.

Far too often in my view, employers of expatriate staff spend a great deal of money in briefing new expatriates about the conditions they are likely to find when abroad whilst, at the same time totally ignoring the fiscal and financial implications which the expatriate will have to face.

Time and time again expatriates get into the most awesome fiscal and financial difficulties because of this attitude by some employers and non-financially orientated commentators on expatriate affairs. Such an attitude implies that the expatriate is either working abroad for the love of it or to enhance career prospects.

One definition of the word "career" is "to progress at great speed and without control down hill".

Please do not let that happen to you; nor should you imagine that you can avoid the situation simply by investing the money that you earn abroad without proper advice. I shall deal with that aspect of choosing an adviser in the investment chapter.

Here I want to enter a plea that you choose your tax adviser with as much care as you will choose the person who you hope will make you wealthy.

Tax, particularly UK tax, has a nasty, underhand, almost noiseless way of creeping up on you; usually just about the time when you are congratulating yourself that you are quite well-off.

UK SOCIAL SECURITY AND PENSIONS

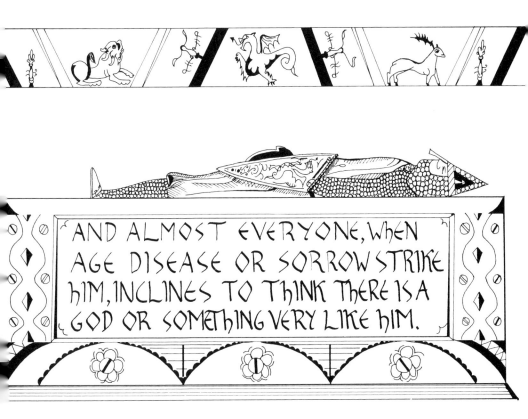

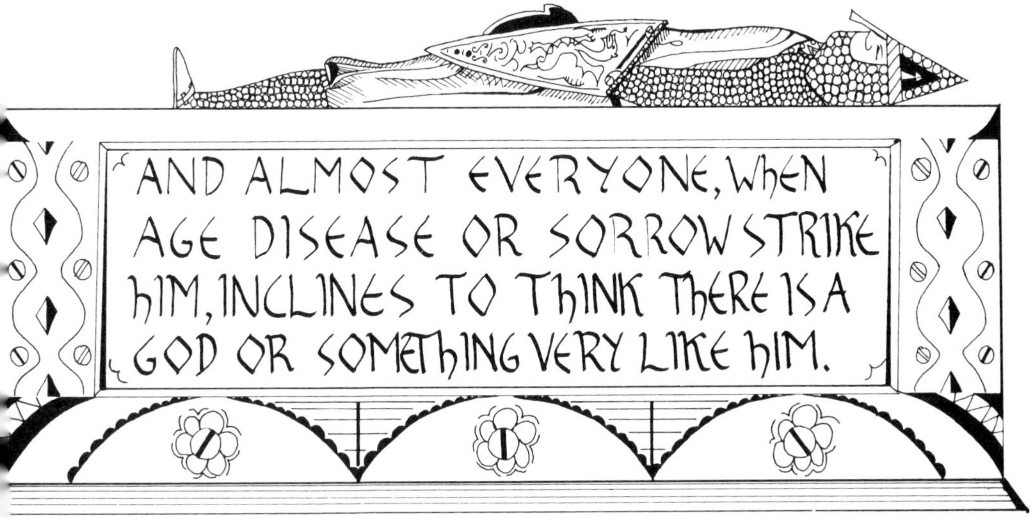

AND ALMOST EVERYONE, WHEN AGE DISEASE OR SORROW STRIKE HIM, INCLINES TO THINK THERE IS A GOD OR SOMETHING VERY LIKE HIM.

None of us is getting any younger; it has been known for a period of working overseas to speed the ageing process! In order for retirement to be entered into smoothly a great deal of planning has to be undertaken.

It is reckoned that there are half a million retired British expatriates in Spain alone. Add to that number all those expats who have retired to Andorra, Cyprus, France, Malta and Portugal and accept that many of them have not taken proper professional advice prior to expatriation; then include the estimated 20,000 new British expatriates who will leave the UK over the next six months and you will see the need for Harry Brown's next book.

RETIRING ABROAD?

Everything that anyone will want to know about taking the decision, packing, removals, taxation, social security, banking, investment, health and the legal aspects of buying property in any of the six major expatriate retirement areas of the world.

Written in Harry Brown's inimitable, easy to read, informed, and authoritative style overseas and UK editions of "Retiring Abroad?" will be published simultaneously by EXPATXTRA LIMITED and NORTHCOTE HOUSE PUBLISHERS LIMITED on 31st March 1987.

Estimates have been made which suggest that around 2,500 working expatriates a month stop working abroad intent on retiring to spend the rest of their lives back in the UK, in parts of the world which have established themselves as retirement areas or to spend summers in the UK and winters in warmer climes.

Often the intentions of many retirees are thwarted by a total lack of planning or, if some planning has been undertaken, by misunderstanding either the fiscal implications or the financial requirements, or both.

For some reason many working British expatriates assume, quite wrongly, that they can play "silly beggars" with the tax laws both of the UK [and the country in which they may spend some of their retirement years] or that they will live quite comfortably for twenty years or more from the income earned from £75,000 of capital accumulated from working abroad.

Quite where such assumptions spring from is a matter for conjecture; rumours on all sorts of matters abound within the working British expatriate community. Regrettably most of the rumours are ill-founded; **practically all the areas which have built up a reputation for being the ideal place to which to retire charge tax on the world wide income and capital gains of their residents** so that capital appreciation and unearned income from investments must almost always be considered as "net" rather than "gross" figures.

Just as important is the fact that, although great strides are being taken throughout the civilised world to lessen the erosion of capital by inflation, prices of goods and services do rise. Some forethought will surely show that it is stretching credulity to the limits for a couple in their mid-fifties to purchase a retirement home in Spain, say, and expect to live comfortably for the rest of their lives on capital of £75,000.

Spain, just like Portugal, France and other retirement areas, charges to tax the world wide incomes and capital gains of its residents. Just as does the UK. It is little or no use leaving investments or interest bearing bank accounts "hidden" off-shore of the country to which you intend to retire unless a] you recognise that you will have to declare income and capital appreciation for tax purposes or b] you intend to live in contravention of the regulations until you die or the authorities discover your "oversight" and penalise you.

Tax apart, the costs of rates, services such as water supply and electricity, running a car, repairs to, and up-keep of, property all have to be taken into account. So a great deal of thought has to be applied, and applied early, to prevent a dream of retiring and doing nothing, other than sit in the sun or fiddle in the garden, becoming a nightmare of scrimping and scraping.

There is no easy answer. Unfair as it might seem after a spell of working hard abroad facts have to be faced. It is nigh-on impossible for anyone to retire in his mid-fifties without either substantial capital upon which to base his future or a pension plan providing him with a sufficient, regular and basic income upon which to live.

The easiest and most reliable pension income plan for any working British expatriate to contribute to is that provided by the UK Social Security system.

And yet what does research reveal?

Less than forty per cent of those 30,000 expatriates who retire each year have bothered to continue contributions to UK Social Security; they seem to regard it as a tax which, since they can in the main avoid it, ought at all costs to be avoided.

It cannot be denied that Social Security contributions are tantamount to a tax; neither can it be denied that most expatriates can avoid paying the contributions. Equally, it cannot be denied that those who take this attitude are foolish in the extreme since they are overlooking the basic fact that when anyone stops working, income of any sort, is well worth having. Particularly, as with UK State pension, when that income is linked to the cost of living index, it can be paid abroad and, if paid abroad, is not subjected to UK tax at source.

UK Social Security

When anyone leaves the UK to work abroad **but remains in the employ of a UK-based company** then, for the first 52 weeks he is abroad, Class 1 social security contributions continue to be levied on the whole of his earnings; just as if he were working in the UK; **provided**

a] **he is ordinarily resident in the UK** and

b] **immediately prior to the start of the overseas assignment he was ordinarily resident there** and

c] **his employer has a place of business in the UK** and

d] **he is not going abroad to work in a country with whom the UK has a reciprocal agreement on social security payments.**

These agreements — a list of the participating countries appears later — regard payment of contributions made to the overseas country as a payment made to the UK social security system.

For DHSS purposes the term **ordinarily resident** covers anyone who intends to return to the UK within three years.

Just like the UK tax implications of going to work overseas the social security regulations can appear, to say the least, somewhat complicated.

Perhaps even more so on the face of it since rarely does a UK-based employee ever have any direct dealings with the Department of Health and Social security. He is used to having occasional cheerful exchanges with the Inland Revenue; the DHSS tends to remain in the background for most of the time.

So, in order to clarify the position of someone who works abroad for a UK employer, let us take a few examples. Alan Able, who appeared in the tax section will serve as the first.

Alan, remember, went to work in Dubai for a period of three years; his employers were based in Manchester.

For the first 52 weeks of his secondment overseas his firm would have continued to pay

Class 1 social security contributions just as though he had turned up for work at their Manchester offices each day. After the first 52 weeks they would not have had any requirement to continue contributions; and neither would Alan. Although, as I shall explain, Alan might [if he were wise he **would**] *decide to pay a voluntary contribution in order to maintain certain benefits for later in his life.*

If, after the first 52 weeks of his secondment to work overseas, Alan had unwisely returned to the UK on paid leave for a period which exceeded 26 weeks [183 days, which would have put him in hot water with the Revenue!] then his liability to make **Class 1** contributions would have reverted for the period of his stay.

The DHSS might further insist that when he returns to Dubai he pays a further 52 weeks Class 1 contribution from the date of his return.

While working in Dubai Alan requires someone to help him and meets another engineer who has been working on a project in Dubai for the previous five years.

Dan Dare is taken onto the UK payroll of Alan's Manchester based employers; he earns just a little less than Alan. He is as British as Alan and intends at the end of the new contract to return to the UK since Alan's employers have offered him a home-based job at the end of the installation contract in Dubai.

Despite the fact that the UK firm is employing him on much the same terms as they are employing Alan they will **not** have to pay Class 1 contributions for him since immediately prior to the start of his overseas assignment he was not resident in the UK. Were Dan to return to the UK on paid leave for a period of more than 26 weeks then he too would have had to pay not only the tax penalty of his foolishness but also Class 1 contributions to the DHSS; just like Alan.

It is very likely that the Manchester firm will prefer the conditions under which Dan Dare's social security contributions are paid since they will not be required to cough-up Class 1 contributions which from 6th October 1985 have forced the employers to pay a percentage of emoluments with **no upper limit!.** In other words, when they were employing Alan back in the UK they had to pay contributions as a percentage of his UK salary [£12,000, say] but once he is abroad on an emoluments package of £100,000 [or more] their contributions are based on that figure. Alan is costing them a fortune for the first 52 weeks; Dan is costing them nothing in social security contributions.

We need to look at two other possible combinations; so two more examples.

Edward East, employed by a UK based firm for many years, is asked to transfer to their office in New Zealand. There will be **no** *liability on his employer's behalf to pay Class 1 contributions for the first 52 weeks of his period abroad because the UK has a reciprocal social security agreement with New Zealand.*

The final example rounds off the possibilities.

Frank Fox, after fifteen years working in the UK, accepts a tempting job offer to go to work in Saudi Arabia for a wholly local firm who have no place of business in the United Kingdom. They agree to pay his salary, in sterling, through their bankers in London.

*Frank, although immediately prior to his overseas appointment he was resident in the UK, will **not** be subjected to the Class 1 contribution rule for the first 52 weeks of his employment abroad since his employers have no place of business in the UK.*

However, Frank, like Dan Dare and Alan Able, might consider it wise to pay voluntary contributions to the UK social security system in order to maintain certain benefits which he might otherwise lose entirely or, at least receive in a diminished amount, when he returns to the UK.

By paying, totally voluntarily as I say, Class 2 or 3 contributions Frank can retain his full entitlement to the basic State retirement pension, sickness benefit*, invalidity pension and allowance, widow's benefit, maternity allowances* and death grant.

Note* sickness benefit and maternity allowances are only preserved if Class 2 contributions are maintained.

He can, since he has no liability to Class 1 contributions, voluntarily pay the lower rate contribution straight away.

Dan Dare and Alan Able will, if they are wise, arrange to make the voluntary contributions during the period of their expatriation **after the first 52 weeks.**

Like Frank they can best do so by appointing an agent in the UK who, put in funds, will pay the contributions in their absence. Such an agent is not mandatory; the DHSS will happily send a request for the contributions to the working expatriate at his overseas address but to my mind the route via the agent is the better one. Firstly because he/she is in the UK [a bank, a relative, a friend makes an ideal paying agent] and therefore there is less likelihood of postal delays. Secondly because, in my experience at least, expatriates tend not to like to part with money even if it is to their ultimate benefit to do so. Voluntary contributions have to be paid on time; time, tides and the DHSS wait for no man!

Far be it from me to suggest to anyone that he should pay a tax when he does not have to; DHSS contributions are, fundamentally a tax as I have said; but they are a tax from which direct benefits can be seen to accrue.

But I regard as foolish in the extreme the attitude of many working expatriates who, after leaving the UK and having the opportunity to continue contributions, spurn doing so. The potential benefits from social security contributions far outweigh the cost of the voluntary payments. Particularly so when you remember that any expatriate, working abroad for a UK employer and at the same time remaining "ordinarily resident" for DHSS purposes, may by paying the voluntary contribution claim **unemployment benefit** if he needs to once he has returned to the UK.

It is a sad fact of modern life that however highly paid he might be whilst abroad, however essential to his employer he considers himself, many an expatriate returns to the UK full of expectation about his future position only to find that his position is long-stop in the dole queue.

Medical treatment, periods in hospital, visits to a Doctor whilst on leave are not governed by contributions of any sort; all visitors to the UK have, as a right, emergency medical facilities at their call. As I shall point out in the section on insurances, it is somewhat foolish of any expatriate to think that he can return to the UK at a time that suits him to have his bunions, piles or sub-acute appendix removed and that he will immediately find a National Health bed available.

A period spent working overseas invariably expands the wallet; it inevitably expands the expatriate's ego too. He tends to think that because he is "someone" in the overseas community he is able to manipulate the medical and hospitalisation system in the UK to suit himself. As I said in the preface, disillusion makes a lumpy mattress; particularly so if it is on a bed in an understaffed or closed NHS ward.

In any case treatment might well be refused if it were discovered that the only reason for the expatriate's visit was to obtain medical treatment. For non-resident visitors the NHS service provides only "emergency" treatment.

Many expatriates worry, quite un-necessarily, that because they are working abroad their families back home do not have the protection of the facilities provided under the National Health Service in the UK. As I have said **everyone**, whether contributing to the social security system or not, is entitled as a right to the treatment and advice provided under the service.

I have included a flow-chart which should lead you through some of the complications; it should help you decide whether you have any mandatory liability to continue to pay UK social security contributions whilst you are abroad. You will see that in very special instances [working in the United States for a limited period, or as a self employed person performing some duties in the UK] Class 1 and Class 4 contributions can be required to be paid; generally though, voluntary Class 2 or 3 contributions are all that can be paid after the first 52 weeks of expatriation.

Just as in tax matters, a person's individual circumstances can alter DHSS generalities. Before going to work overseas or, whilst overseas and having doubts about any liability to contributions, you should consult the **Overseas Branch, Department of Health and Social Security, Newcastle upon Tyne, NE98 1YX.**

However well-organised and helpful the staff in Overseas Branch of the DHSS are you should realise that they can only be so if you help them. Quote your UK Social Security number when you write; sometimes expatriates get confused as to which of many "official" tags they ought refer.

You may have medical reference numbers which look like ACDE 173 3 or ZN 91 41 03 D.

It is the second of these two that the DHSS wants; but please do not use either of those which I have quoted; they are mine!

Child Benefit

Entitlement to continuing UK child benefit is determined by several factors.

a] Anyone who goes abroad to work accompanied by his children will stop receiving child benefit unless he is going to a country with whom the UK has a

reciprocal agreement. In which case either the UK benefit may be claimed or the benefit of the "host" country becomes payable.

b] In most EEC countries whether your children are with you there or not you will be eligible to claim that country's child benefit [in many instances benefit much higher than that paid in the UK]. If you are self employed within the EEC the children must be with you in order for the benefit to be claimable.

c] Any servant of the UK Crown [army personnel, teachers employed by the Crown but working overseas] continues to have his overseas emoluments taxed in the UK how ever long he works abroad. In such cases child benefit is claimable even though the child might be abroad for the whole time.

In most other cases eligibility for child benefit ceases immediately if you intend to go abroad to work for more than eight weeks and take your children with you. If, as is quite common, a family waits in the UK for a time whilst the husband/father works abroad then child benefit may be claimed until the family joins him.

In order to assess your eligibility or otherwise to continuing child benefit you should, if you are in any doubts, write to the **DHSS Information Division, Leaflet Unit, Block 4, Government Buildings, Honeypot Lane, Stanmore, Middlesex HA7 1AY.** If you are still in the UK and considering a move abroad then you may ask your local DHSS office for leaflet CH6 and form CH181 [TO].

Private Pension Planning

I have already stressed the fact that the simplest way in which to secure some pension is via the state scheme; many expatriates, particularly those working abroad for UK based firms, will belong to an employer-sponsored scheme. They may be contributing to that scheme; they may receive the benefits of the scheme without any contributions on their part.

Rather more than half the working British expatriate population work either on contract for UK employers who provide no pension arrangements or for truly foreign employers who either provide no pension entitlement at all or who provide schemes based in the foreign country.

Whatever his particular situation any working British expatriate is faced with pension problems rather more complex and certainly different from those faced by his UK-based counterpart.

If he is a member of a company-sponsored plan it might be a "local" plan subjected to that country's exchange control regulations; difficulties might arise in having the pension remitted to him once benefit begins.

If he is without any employer support he has to face the financial headaches of planning for retirement with only the schemes available to him from a few financial institutions.

In order to start pension planning additional to any state pension a number of matters have to be considered.

1] What is your normal retirement date?

2] To which country's social security system are you contributing and does that country have a reciprocal agreement with the UK?

3] Are you in a company sponsored pension plan?

4] If so does it provide a pension related to your service and final salary?

5] If the employer's scheme does relate to your final salary is this your *total* salary or just your base salary [your emoluments less the "extras" you receive for working overseas]?

If you are not in an employer's pension scheme and have to make your own provision, you can start by determining some of the answers yourself; for example, when do you intend to retire? Take my advice and do not make that date too early unless you intend to save a considerable amount of money between now and then!

Once the answers to these questions have been reached a base for pension planning emerges. You will begin to have some clue as to where your pension is going to come from and when it is likely to be paid.

The next question to be answered is the big one.

How much?!!!

In the UK it is generally thought that the best level for your pension is two-thirds of your final salary plus the social security pension. This two-thirds figure is not necessarily the ideal; it has become the "norm" because it is roughly the equivalent to a full Civil Service pension. It is also the maximum [perchance I am sure] that the Inland Revenue [doyens of the Civil Service] will approve under a company pension plan.

In most cases the two-thirds limit bears little relevance to a person's financial needs in retirement; these needs will be governed by many other things such as income tax, outstanding debts [such as mortgage], the need to go on providing for young children by way of school fees etc. It is also "normal" for the pension to reduce by fifty per cent on the death of the employee; normally the man. The widow's pension is therefore quite dramatically reduced.

But what if the husband is twenty or thirty years older than his wife? Will he [will she!] be happy to think that she might have to survive him by a decade or two on half of what they were together receiving during his retirement period?

It is far better to look closely at the net income needs in retirement rather than at what some outdated and totally impersonal legislation predetermines.

As a rule of thumb it is far better to aim for eighty per cent of net income prior to retirement and that this should be designed to escalate during the course of payment in order to keep pace with inflation. Remember that if you are going to retire abroad, especially to a country where inflation might be higher than in the UK, the inflation factor might be something that will demand a great deal of thought.

The expatriate who proposes to retire to the UK **must** remember that all forms of income, including pension's income, are aggregated to produce the gross taxable income; unearned income and pensions income are treated as a pool into which the Revenue dip their bucket. The only relief available in this area is for expatriates who have pensions related to foreign service from a foreign source; in which instance only ninety per cent of the pension is taken into account for this purpose.

Once the target has been determined the next step is to try to work out the weapon with which you intend to hit the bull.

The very first bullet is social security.

I have said it before, I shall say it again, contributing to social security is a must. Not a maybe, a perhaps or "I'll get round to it some day" idea but a now, an imperative, an "I must do it now or for ever regret it" **MUST.**

You should determine to which country's state pension you will be entitled and whether there will be any "block" on its payment; if it is coming from a foreign country does that country have a double tax treaty with the country to which you are retiring? Does it deduct tax at source? The likelihood is that only a pensions expert will be able to help resolve these answers.

In the UK a non-expatriate employee with a full contribution record can expect to get a basic pension [currently £3,187.60 per annum for a married man] plus, either from his company plan or the state [if he is contracted "into" the state scheme] an earnings related pension equal to 1.25 per cent of earnings between £3,187.60 and £13,780 per annum for each year of contribution up to a maximum of twenty years. In other words for a full contribution record the UK social security system provides a pension roughly equal to twenty five per cent of earnings up to a "ceiling" of £13,780 per annum, and this is inflation protected too.

Remember that although this pension is only available from age 65 [for men] and 60 [for women] it forms a large "chunk" of money for which the expatriate would otherwise have to fund privately: the expatriate who refuses [stupidly], is unable [regrettably], or fails [accidentally] to recognise the role that the UK's state system provides must live with the consequences.

The eighty per cent target which I have suggested can also play havoc with the calculations of any expatriate whose pension from his UK employer is geared to his "notional" UK salary; a salary which will undoubtedly be very much lower than the salary which he is earning abroad.

As it is your actual notional salary that is producing your current standard of living the cut-back at retirement is likely to produce some nasty shocks at retirement.

Where ever you work, whether back in the UK or as an expatriate, the most difficult point for any pensions consultant to get across will be that it is never too early to start saving for your retirement.

I accept that anyone in his twenties or thirties [or if he is that insensitive, in his forties or fifties] might find it hard to recognise the fact that one day his chosen profession will have to get along without him. Marriage, mortgages and babies [sometimes not in that order] tend to get in the way of long term planning. Sometimes grown up children's marriages, mortgages and babies [sometimes not in that order either] tend to make demands on current income, leaving little for future planning.

Do try, very hard, to keep retirement in perspective; try not to consign planning for it into the "one day I must get down to doing something about this" pile.

It is a fact of life that the earlier you start to set aside money for retirement the less you will have to dig into your reserves later and the lower your "contribution" rate will have to be now. And now is when you can probably afford more.

Let us consider an employee on a starting salary of £10,000 at various ages and assume that this salary will grow at five per cent per annum. He, or he plus his employer, is going to pay contributions to buy him a pension at, say, age 60 of two thirds of his final salary. We shall imagine that these contributions are going to be invested to give a return of 12 per cent per annum.

The table below shows the percentage of salary required to produce this pension on these factors.

Age	Retirement pension p.a.	% of salary required
30	£28,814	9.05
35	£22,576	12.54
40	£17,689	17.72
45	£13,860	26.81
50	£10,860	43.21

Bear in mind that in each case it has been assumed that the starting salary at the age shown is £10,000 per annum; if higher salaries are taken the percentage of contributions from salary goes up more steeply. And remember that this table aims at pensions of two thirds final salary; not the eighty per cent which I have suggested should be the ideal target.

An expatriate who is not paying tax in the UK will not get tax relief to his contributions to any UK arrangement but could, if he overlooks this incentive, get the other advantages of tax free accumulation by making additional voluntary contributions to any scheme set up by his UK based employer. The question to be asked is "are there any better alternatives?" It has to be remembered that there are strict limits to the amount of tax free commutation which can be taken from a UK based pension arrangement.

Setting up an "off-shore" arrangement might give the individual expatriate [whether he is also a member of a UK scheme or not] far greater freedom of choice. He would be able to determine not only whether he takes the whole or none of his off-shore accumulations in a lump sum but also decide how and where he would like his pension paid. Several international firms recognise this extra freedom and run special pensions arrangements off-shore of the UK in order that their foreign-based British staff can enjoy the extra benefits. If the idea appeals to the employers it ought appeal to you.

Even if you intend to return to the UK to resume tax residence and employment with your UK employer an off-shore facility is still a good idea. Free of UK tax you will be able to "import" the cash from the off-shore scheme and buy "back service" years from your employer's scheme.

As I have said the pension's law of the UK has, to a very large extent, been determined by comparison to what legislators have considered to be the ideal; basically that ideal has been founded on the pension accrued by a long standing civil servant.

In the main residents of the UK have to live with both the advantages and the strictures that the legislation produces. Whilst recognising the advantages you have also to recognise the strictures. If you are currently employed abroad by a UK firm at a notional salary for pension purposes of £20,000 per annum whilst actually enjoying an overseas salary of £40,000 you will, even if you receive a full two thirds pension of UK base salary, actually receive, by way of pension, one third of the salary upon which you have been basing your life style. You must also, surely, recognise the fact that your dependents will also suffer a diminution of financial support at your death.

If your wife is considerably younger than you, if you have young children who will rely on you for a decade or so, then additional pension planning is a must. Pension planning hopefully allied to some of the life insurance plans which I have outlined in the insurance chapter; policies designed to protect your family against your untimely death rather than to provide for your own retirement.

As I have said, you may have a wife very much younger than you; working abroad can create all sorts of difficulties in marital relationships and second marriages are far from rare.

Married to a woman a decade or two younger, many men in their forties and fifties find themselves having to think very hard about pension entitlement and benefits to dependents since they have a second "crop" of children. The UK-based schemes rarely take account of this; off-shore plans can be totally bespoke; fitting exactly rather than simply where they touch.

Personal pension schemes designed specifically for the working British expatriate community are now available from a number of major off-shore insurance companies; primarily those who are off-shoots of reputable and established unit trust managers. Companies such as Eagle Star, Save and Prosper, Lloyd's Life, Equity and Law and Providence Capitol, all with long-held and hard-earned reputations in investment management, provide such plans. Each is a little different from the other; each has its advantages, each its disadvantages.

I have to say that I do not think that, as yet anyway, any of them has come up with the ideal plan. That statement will probably get me into some hot water but if it does then my splashing about might improve what is available or encourage another investment house to look closely at plans it might be thinking of introducing in the pensions field.

Unless you have some specialised knowledge in this esoteric area your interests will be best served by engaging a consultant with the knowledge you lack.

That consultant should not only be interested in how much you can save towards retirement each year but your particular needs for help; you may have a child who, through some disability, will be dependent upon you long past the age of eighteen; a child who might well remain financially dependent upon the family "store cupboard"

long after you and your wife are dead. He will consider with you your intentions to retire abroad, the tax strictures which might be imposed upon you by those aims, the currency in which your pension plans might be denominated and the score of other allied but important matters which you might otherwise overlook.

Pension planning is for to-day; whilst you are still earning and whilst you can still divert some savings into this important area.

It is not a matter which can be left until a year or two before you aim to retire; at whatever age and whatever place you intend to spend those more relaxed years the longer time you can devote to designing your retirement aims the better.

I have tried to point out that failing to keep up social security contributions is a big mistake; to that I would add one further error. However short a time you work abroad outside the protection of a pension scheme you will weaken the foundations which underpin your financial future unless you set aside some money for retirement.

Most investment houses who produce plans for retirement funding recognise that fact and have evolved schemes into which a couple of year's "premiums" or a lump sum might be injected. You invest with them whilst you are able and leave the accrued savings to grow on a long term plan; aiming for capital appreciation over a considerable number of years.

A competent pensions adviser will know which plans are suitable for you and, in the light of your individual circumstances will be able to help shape your future by designing for you the right combination of plans. As in practically every chapter of this book I caution you about trying to do so without professional advice.

There is an old musical hall song which my Mum used to sing to me when I was a child [she still would if I asked her I suspect] which, although referring to a much earthier matter, has a refrain that sums up the attitude you ought take with pensions planning.

"Do you know it, can you tell me?
Would somebody be kind enough to say?
Do you know it, can you tell me
'Cos, I'd do it if I only knew the way!"

UK Social Security Contributions

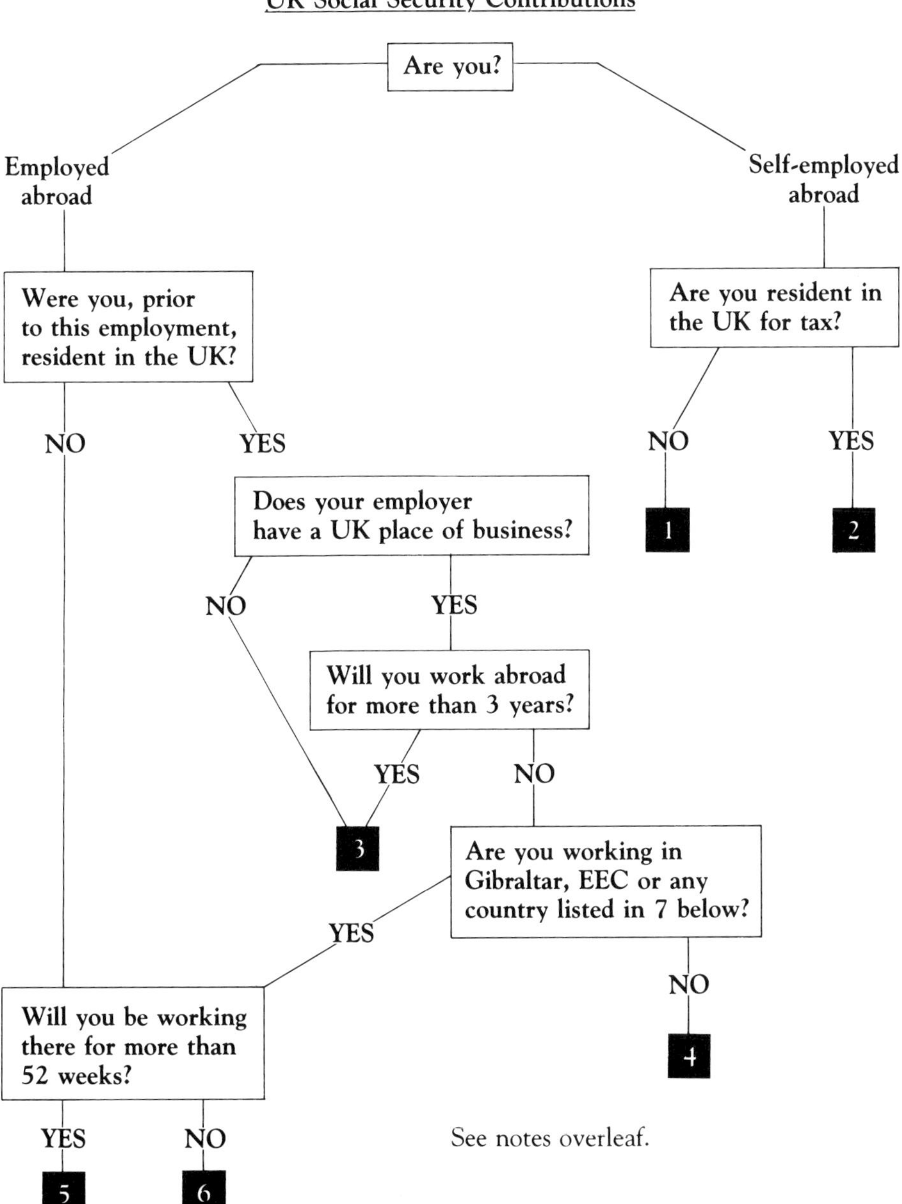

See notes overleaf.

NOTES

1 you are eligible to pay class 4 contributions plus class 2 contributions for any week you work in the UK.
2 you have no UK DHSS liabilities but may pay class 2 or 3 contributions voluntarily.
3 you have no UK DHSS liabilities but may pay class 2 or 3 contributions voluntarily.
4 you are liable to class 1 contributions for the first 52 weeks after which you may pay class 2 or 3 voluntarily.
5 you have no liability to UK contributions.
6 you are liable for class 1 contributions throughout your period of work abroad.

The United Kingdom has reciprocal agreements with the following countries:

Australia	Malta
Austria	New Zealand
Bermuda	Norway
Canada	Spain
Cyprus	Sweden
Finland	Switzerland
Guernsey	Turkey
Israel	United States
Jamaica	Yugoslavia
Jersey	all EEC countries

SAVINGS AND INVESTMENT

YOU'VE GOT TO KNOW WHEN TO HOLD'EM
KNOW WHEN TO FOLD'EM
KNOW WHEN TO WALK AWAY
KNOW WHEN TO RUN.

The next few lines of the song from which the excerpt is taken go on to warn "Never count your money when you're sitting at the table; there'll be time enough for counting when the dealing's done".

It's where the investment connoisseur keeps his readies.

It's called the NatWest Special Reserve Account.

It's new. It's rather select.

And all you need to take advantage of it is a NatWest Current Account, plus £2,000 or more to invest. (After that, £250 is the minimum deposit or withdrawal.)

On the one hand, you'll enjoy all the benefits of a higher investment account.

Yet of the other, you can make withdrawals through your Current Account without any advance notice. This allows your investment to earn interest in full, right up until the last minute. What's more, any Current Account linked to a Special Reserve Account will be free of the normal account charge. Provided it's in credit, of course. All of which leaves just one question.

Why isn't your money enjoying the same privileges?

It's reassuring to know that your investment is always at the ready.

For indication rates and further information please write to:

The Manager,
National Westminster Bank plc,
PO Box No. 20,
23 Broad Street,
St. Helier, Jersey,
Channel Islands.

Once upon a time it was the sole financial objective of many members of the working British expatriate community to pour money into building societies; despite the fact that the interest was subject to a UK tax imposition which was not reclaimable by non-residents. Expatriates took this step largely because, at that time, they could do little else; there was not much of the more sophisticated financial industry which has been developed to explore the vast potential that expatriates have for earning, saving, banking, investing and occasionally wasting money.

Now that industry has a new and powerful member; building societies, whilst providing a safe and well respected haven for savings, now compete with the banks to provide interest-bearing accounts the interest of which can be paid gross to persons **not ordinarily resident** within the UK. If their past achievements are anything to go by it will not be long before the building societies are making big in-roads into accounts which banks and investment houses thought their sole prerogative.

Are we soon to see them move into providing certain financial services "off-shore" of the UK; services directed at the working British expatriate community?

It could be; although, since societies were held at the starting gate for far longer than they should have been, the banks and fund managers have a head start. Will that worry the building societies?

The performance record of several off-shore investment managers leaves much to be desired. The less active, less caring money managers could be accused of being a mite too eager to promote their advantageous tax position and none too worried about the enhancement in the value of expatriates' cash vouchsafed to their charge. There are more than one [in fact "more than one" several dozen times over] fund managers who would hardly be able to say that putting money in a building society was "foolish" if the return on an investment with them was carefully compared to the record of the building societies over the years. And now the societies can claim a measure of tax efficiency in accounts they hold for some expatriates those fund managers will really have to look to their laurels; provided they know where they are!

How much can you set aside each month?

The favourite question of investment salesmen which, for a while at least, a new expatriate should parry.

Whatever form of investment or savings scheme is envisaged it is hardly likely that in the first few months of his posting the new expatriate will have either the time or the inclination to determine how much of his excess salary can be saved. It is very unusual for anyone to go to work abroad without having commitments of some kind back home; wife and family to support, perhaps; outstanding financial liabilities to banks or charge cards [or both!] to be paid off as quickly as possible.

There ought to be two deterrents to beginning any investment programme too early. The first is that until any expatriate is convinced that his overseas emoluments are safe from erosion by UK tax impositions he ought to remain firmly fixed in cash. If he begins to get involved in contractural investment plans allied to unit trusts [be they authorised trusts in the UK or the more non-resident oriented funds offshore] then he could find, if he needs to return to the UK prematurely or infringes the UK tax law, that he is without sufficient cash to pay his tax liabilities. Most contractual investment schemes [particularly those linked to life policies] provide the most minimal of cash in the form of surrender values for many years. So it must make sense for any expatriate to ensure that until he is free of any nasty tax shocks his excess earnings are readily available in a bank or building society account.

It will do him no harm to be in cash for a while; returns may not be great but they are assured. Even if, hopefully, he can establish himself as fully non-resident and free from a UK tax liability on his overseas emoluments he will have calculated just how much he can save with ease before entering savings plans which demand regular "premiums" or monthly payments in order to secure their benefits. There are often advantages in putting a lump sum, single premium into such plans; so little will be lost other than the eager salesman's commission.

The other deterrent will be something that affects most, if not all expatriates; a sort of psychological condition that I have named "*expatriatitis*". The symptoms are the sudden realisation that you have the ability to earn more money than you have ever earned before; the ability to look at goods like cameras, hi-fi, word-processors and jewellery and not have to walk away from them since using the "funny money" in which you are being paid does not seem like spending; more like a game.

In the early days of expatriation that is how it should be viewed; as a game. One day, when I have more time, I am going to invent a board game which intending expatriates will be able to play before they leave the UK. It will consist of giving them piles of coloured paper and shuffling cards depicting all the highly desirable but totally un-necessary objects available in souks, hyper-markets and duty free shops. The object of the game will be to see who can spend his money fastest in the collection of the most frivolous objects. The winner will make the best expatriate!

Expatriatitis is a condition which is rarely fatal provided that the symptoms persist for no more than the first six months of expatriation. In which sad event the only cure is to get a good grip on yourself and give yourself a good talking to; it is a cure that no professional can effect; a spouse maybe, but the likelihood is that, since the condition can be contagious within a family unit [even if the family is 2,000 miles or more away] self-treatment is the only way. And expatriatitis serves a practical purpose; it indicates a budgeting capability. After six months simply sit down and add up the cost of the Nikon F3, the Bang & Olufsen and the 22 carat bracelets, divide the total by six and you have some idea of what you can afford to save. It will give you a breathing space, make the early days abroad tolerable, and serve the very pragmatic purpose of showing you just how much money you will be able to save from your earnings.

Any investment adviser worthy of the name will be conscious of your priorities, real or imagined, and welcome for your sake the chance you are taking of getting your savings and investment act together. It is wholly undesirable that any new expatriate should commit himself to a fixed savings plan or investment programme for this period. Until the pattern of his life has been established, until the hay making has come to an end it is totally foolhardy to instigate any such programme.

Few bank managers, fund managers or caring professional advisers will try to talk you into contractural plans too early; if one does regard him with suspicion. There **are** other bank managers, fund managers and professional advisers; try one of them instead.

Also disregard any advice that you receive on investment matters from other expatriates; most certainly during the period of expatriatitis and, quite possibly, for the remainder of your expatriate life. In expatriate communities there are only two things that spread faster than unsound advice on savings and investment matters; one is unsound advice on UK tax matters and so is the other! Unless the advice comes from an existing expatriate who has already got his knees brown **and** has professional qualifications and experience then ignore him.

It must also be said that there are numerous itinerant salesmen who ply their investment wares in the countries in which the majority of British expatriates work overseas. It is very difficult for the newcomer to distinguish between the representatives of reputable firms and others who have little more than a glib sales pitch and an interest in their commission earning capabilities.

The fund managers and insurance companies who carefully design products to cope with working expatriates' requirements are all too keenly aware that "policing" the undesirable element is difficult. That difficulty does not stop them trying; it is likely that even more measures to sort the wheat from the chaff will be adopted. But you must be wary. By all means listen to what the salesman has to say, consider with him the products he has to offer and question him closely about his firm's standing in the expatriate market. See how long the firm has been established, look at the pedigree of the institution whose plans or policies he is promoting; no professional will mind your doing that. And if you are at all uneasy about the advice you are receiving commit yourself to nothing until you have checked him out. If necessary write to the fund manager or life assurance company direct; address your letter to the International Marketing Director of the institution involved and see whether his assessment of the performance of the product on offer is the same as the salesman's and whether he, the Marketing Director, feels that the product is as appropriate to your needs as the salesman seems to think it is.

Please do not imagine that I am condemning all itinerant salesmen.

Itinerant, according to my dictionary, implies that the salesman will travel from one place to another, remaining only in one location for a short period.

Even the most reputable, distinguished of institutions such as long established banks, insurance companies and fund managers send out representatives who can only be on foreign locations for a relatively short time. I have more than a sneaking feeling that representatives from building societies will soon be joining them too.

Experts normally practise their professions from a UK or Channel Islands base or internationally-oriented specialists who practise from Switzerland, Gibraltar, the Isle of Man, Bermuda or the Netherlands. They must, perforce, all travel into and out of a country quite quickly; it is vital to their understanding of the expatriate's needs that they see for themselves the situation "on the ground". They need to practise their skills outside their own offices. An abdominal surgeon who is always to be found sitting with his plump hands across his plump tummy in his plush Harley Street consulting rooms would not be my first choice were I suddenly to need my appendix removed. I would prefer the practical sort; the guy who gets his rubber gloves messy very regularly. Practice makes perfect and when it is my money or my appendix at stake I like the practitioner rather than the theoretician.

How should anyone go about choosing an adviser?

Before going to work abroad the chances are that a man had little or no need of financial advice; his banking was restricted to watching the diminishing balance of his current account; his investment and life assurance needs dictated by what little he could afford out of a restrictive and restricting budget.

Now, with money burning a hole in his bank account, an expatriate may have no clue as to his requirements or need of advice on specific subjects. Previously his dealings with the Inland Revenue might have consisted of completing a tax return once in a while and paying his income tax under the PAYE system. The major part of his life assurance and pensions plans, his medical and hospitalisation insurances might all have been provided by his employer; now he might be on a "go it alone basis".

If he is then his understanding of life policies or medical insurances, capital gains tax on investments, currencies other than sterling, and a thousand other matters to which expatriate flesh is heir, might be sadly lacking. He will, of course, not know what his deficiences are.

His adviser should; and not be scared of pointing them out; even if his client, the expatriate, is somewhat loth to feel that the advice is totally pertinent.

So my first suggestion is never to go along with an adviser who constantly agrees with what you want to do. He could be as unskilled in investment matters as you are.

Next, ask around. Not necessarily amongst your compatriot expatriates; in fact rarely amongst your compatriot expatriates.

We all make mistakes and high on the list of those made by expatriates is that of choosing an adviser on financial matters; none of us likes openly to admit to our mistakes. We all tend to disguise our personal assessment of the efficacy of advisers in an attempt to suggest that we chose wisely.

Ask your bank manager of what he knows of "the XYZ Fund Managers Ltd". Write to the Marketing Director of the fund managers in which you are interested and ask to see copies of the balance sheets, current brochures, future investment strategy etc.

Write to the professional institutions of which a prospective adviser might be a member.

You would not hand out good, hard earned money to someone you met in the street just because you liked the look of him and he handed over some highly coloured share certificates which might contain highly coloured promises of financial security.

Consider every step very carefully and be rushed into nothing by no-one. In financial matters he who hesitates is usually thinking about it; and that is the sign of an intelligent man.

Think long, think hard and act slowly until you have the measure of the person who is intent on selling you something.

Every one you meet from an investment house, bank, insurance company, financial adviser, stock-broker, accountancy or legal practice and, now building society, will be trying to sell you something.

That is his job; he too has to earn a living and selling you his services is how he earns it. It will be your fault entirely if you are sold a pup!

Now let us turn our attention to specific opportunities for you to see your money work for you. But before we do let me issue you yet another warning.

I do not know you; you do not know me. I cannot possibly advise you, in a book, about your specific needs. Even if any of the suggestions I offer you fit you like a glove dismiss them as but suggestions. As I pointed out in the tax chapter anyone, even I, can appear clever on paper. Anyone can make exaggerated claims and juggle figures around to prove excellence or incompetence.

The first of himself and the second of others.

In this book I am personally trying to sell you nothing. Mind you, I did try by overseeing the artwork of the cover, which was designed to attract the attention of potential purchasers. I know nothing about cover design [to be frank I cannot draw a straight line along a ruler] so I went to an adviser. With his help I have attracted you to buy this book and there my commercial attitude stops; I could not, from a monetary point of view, care less whether you take any notice of what I say about banking or investment. I just hope that something of what I say proves useful to you. The role of the adviser is to ensure that he is useful.

Bank accounts

Rare will be the expatriate who is not familiar with a **current account.** You put money in the bank; the bank issues you with cheques to allow you to draw it out again to pay bills etc. etc. etc. The bank manager gets edgy or, sometimes, downright rude if you draw out more than you put in. Rare too will be the expatriate who, probably before he became an expatriate, has not received a letter from his bank manager that he would rather not have received.

In their very simplest form current accounts are there to prevent you having to carry around with you a suitcase full of notes.

Now-a-days, as competition has grown stronger between banks, current accounts can also earn you a very reasonable amount of interest provided you keep a modest credit balance. Why anyone has an old-style current account is beyond me; especially when the facility to draw on **interest bearing current accounts** is so easy.

So, if you have a non-interest bearing current account and your present bankers have not sent you details of interest bearing current account facilities write to another bank and ask what they have to offer. Once you understand what is available remove your account from your present bankers and put it in the hands of a bank more alive to your needs rather than to their own.

All the major British banks have interest bearing current accounts available to their clients [both expatriates and home-based clients]. It will be a sloppy bank manager who will not have brought these facilities to your notice. Do not put up with a sloppy bank manager!

All the major British banks also have branches off-shore of the United Kingdom; branches in Alderney, Guernsey, the Isle of Man and Jersey. Any one of whom can provide you with exactly the same standard of service as any competent branch in the United Kingdom.

Earlier on I was somewhat scathing about financial institutions who offer expatriates **tax efficiency** and little else. My remarks do not apply to the major members of the off-shore banking fraternity.

They can offer you exactly the same services, rates of interest and types of accounts as can be found in mainland UK branches

a] **always more tax-efficiently provided you are non-resident for UK tax purposes** and

b] **inevitably just as efficiently [often more so] when it comes to providing services to you as an expatriate.**

Off-shore banks in the centres that I have already mentioned are used to dealing with expatriates. They are geared up to dealing with expatriates; expatriates form a major part of their customer force.

Therefore I repeat that all off-shore British banks have more expertise in dealing with expatriates than do their counterparts in the United Kingdom.

They can be more **tax efficient** because of the UK tax laws relating to bank interest which I have already explored in the tax chapter and which get a detailed mention in the Returning Home chapter.

Remember that interest bearing accounts are not all denominated as **deposit**

accounts any longer; a tidy sum in a current account can presently earn a tidy sum in interest. And that interest should be protected from the UK Revenue by your ensuring that such accounts are run from an off-shore base. Interest bearing current accounts also provide the ideal way in which a non-resident husband can share accounts with his resident wife without involving her in too heavy a UK tax liability on her "share" of the interest.

The present single person's personal allowance in the UK is currently £2,335; that would mean that a jointly held interest bearing current account could earn interest of £4,500 a year and still not encourage a UK tax liability. With interest rates moderately low and, seemingly, falling still further, it would be a tidy sum in a current account that attracted over £4,500 of interest every year. The current account would also ensure that if the husband died his wife would be able to draw on the account swiftly rather than await the hassles of probate to release his locked up deposit accounts.

Deposit accounts

Deposit accounts, as their name implies, are accounts in which a sum of money is lodged for some time; that time can be as short as seven days or as long as five years.

You may tell the bank from the outset when you require your deposit to be made available to you again and, in return, the bank will tell you the rate of interest they will pay; adding it to your capital upon the maturity of the deposit.

Or you may tell the bank that they may have the cash for as long as you allow them and they will issue you with what is known as a **"call"** account. You may recall your money by giving an agreed number of days, weeks or months notice of your withdrawal.

If you are sharp — and I am sure that you are — you will compare the rates of interest offered for a fixed term deposit with those offered for a call account requiring you to tell the bank that you are withdrawing your money. You might find that, say, a six month fixed term deposit account attracts x% per annum interest whilst a "call" account requiring you to give six months' notice of withdrawal is offered at x+% per annum.

If six months is an attractive time for you to keep your money with the bank do not simply hand over the cash for the least attractive of the accounts; go for the "call" account. Pay your money over the counter of the bank, open the call account, and tell the banker that you are now "calling" in the return of the cash. In six months' time he will pay you more than you would have got for the fixed term deposit.

A pleasant and totally harmless little game; **but on other matters never play bankers games with bankers!** Especially since you can have deposit accounts and call accounts in **foreign currencies** too.

Unless you have a specific reason for having a dollop of US$ dollars, a packet of pesetas or a mountain of marks available to you at the end of a predetermined period always keep your exposure to currency risks down to the shortest time possible.

It might be very pleasant to be told by a banker that he can offer you 2x% per annum if you deposit cash in Dutch guilders or French francs for a year; it might be a disaster if you accept.

A year is a lifetime in foreign currency dealings. In that time your currency could have increased by 2x% per annum interest and fallen by 10x% per annum in exchange markets.

Believe you me the banker will be out of his exposure to currency risk faster than you can say "I shouldn't oughta done it" and at the end of the twelve months will happily buy stocks of the distressed foreign currency and pay you back in it.

Most bankers are honest as the day is long; they get paid for being honest. They also get paid for being craftier than you are when it comes to dealing in money.

So, no foreign currency accounts just for the hell of it unless you are very very rich, very very clever, or want to be thought either.

If you need to fund for the purchase of a piece of foreign property in foreign currency in a month or two and you have the cash in one currency but require it in another **speak to your trusted banker** before you start any currency dealings. He may suggest to you that in his opinion you will be better making the transaction now, or that you should wait, or buy half now and that the rest should be bought "forward". It is his job to advise you in the light of your circumstances.

As a general rule of thumb remember that handling currencies is a job which requires about as much expertise as handling unexploded World War II bombs found on the roof of a dynamite factory. Except that the bang can be bigger.

The job of every banker is to safeguard his clients' interests at every turn. You should not simply rely upon him to lock your cash in his safe every night. He can provide all sorts of services relating to money; borrowing it, lending it, spending it, saving it and changing it into other types of money. That is his role in life and I know no banker who is unhappy to perform that role to the best of his ability and to the best of his clients' interests; having made sure, of course, that the bank's interests are safeguarded too.

Many expatriates feel that they want to be adventurous rather than just putting money in the bank. They wish to "invest" as well as "save". **Remember that "savings" should always be in cash.** Never in units, stocks, diamonds, stamps or any other commodity which has, hopefully, a cash value.

Commodities, stocks, diamonds, stamps or anything else are worth nothing unless you can persuade someone else to buy them from you; in order to do so he has to have cash.

Make sure just in case you wish to buy something at some time in the future, [the kids' schooling, a new car, a new house, some food, etc] or have to pay a hefty amount of tax that you have some of your excess earnings tucked away in cash. Not in

unit trusts; they have quite a different and important role to play in your overall investment scenario.

All the "high street" banks, apart from their normal branches, have subsidiaries off-shore of the UK who act as deposit taking institutions just as the parent bank does; but rather than being in competition with the parent these firms [normally known as **Finance Companies**] extend the services which the banking group can provide. They can do so because they operate directly into the "money markets" and can, therefore, offer a very flexible deposit taking service which reflects the immediacy of the markets in which they are dealing.

Expatriates often ask whether money deposited with the off-shore off-shoot of a major bank is as safe as that deposited with the parent; after all they are usually under quite distinct management.

All I can ask in return is whether you would seriously expect any high street bank to allow any subsidiary to flounder?

Only once you have a cash deposit should you consider entering any form of investment.

Over the years I have been able to talk with many unit trust and managed fund trust managers. Without exception they have all agreed that the very first requirement that a working expatriate has for his excess earnings is to hold some in cash. So I am not alone in suggesting that before you invest you should save. The real money whizz-kids might not agree; but the sound minded, sober-sided, highly responsible investment managers with millions if not billions of £ sterling or US dollars to "play with" all do.

None that I know of would suggest that anyone should invest with them until he had money in the bank or building society to which he could turn for necessities or in a crisis.

Building Society accounts

Until 6th April, 1986, building society accounts were no-where as attractive — from an expatriate's viewpoint — as were bank deposit accounts. Interest had to be paid to every one, wherever in the world he lived, net of a UK income tax imposition.

Now, not before time, the same facility as the UK banks enjoy is extended to building societies; they may pay interest gross provided that the depositor is **not ordinarily resident** in the UK.

Recent years have seen building societies engage banks in the fight for depositors' money; the banks started selling mortgages quite actively so the building societies sharpened their marketing tools. It is early days yet but they can be expected to enter the expatriate field with the same verve.

To some degree it might be to the building societies' advantage to have had to wait to be attractive to expatriates. Not all that has gone on before they were able to enter the arena has been an overwhelming success. Many banks, many insurance companies and investment houses have made mistakes in the marketing of services and investment products to expatriates.

There has been a tendency to evolve schemes without an in-depth appraisal of the expatriates' needs. Only lately, for example, has any investment manager turned his attention to the provision of pension plans for expatriates; despite the fact that the need has been there for a very long time.

Having sat on the side lines so long, itching to join in, the building societies should have noticed where the holes in the market are and be prepared to provide the necessary services to fill the needs.

The plans currently available from the building societies are all, quite naturally, based on the savings and investment schemes available to the normal, resident-for-UK-tax members of the societies. And there is nothing wrong with that idea; by introducing new plans gradually the societies will be able to build up their experience of the requirements of expatriates.

Provided an existing expatriate member [who previously was somewhat unwise to keep too much money in one of the societies' accounts because of the tax penalty] can now give the society of which he is a member a signed declaration as to his non-resident status he will [until he returns to resume tax residence] receive his interest gross.

An expatriate who has not previously saved with a building society will find that on application to any one of them for details of the schemes a declaration form is included in the marketing material he receives. Until that declaration is in the hands of the building society net interest will have to be paid or credited to the account you set up.

Remember also that it would be very foolish for any expatriate not ordinarily resident in the UK to attempt to share the account with anyone who is resident there. It would totally negate the tax efficiency of the societies' new ability to pay interest gross if one of the signatories to the account [beneficially entitled to the interest accrued or paid] is resident for UK tax purposes.

The declaration which has to be signed points out this requirement and it would be very foolish indeed for any expatriate to ignore it.

So, once again I fear, I have to point out that if you are not ordinarily resident in the UK and your wife is either "technically" resident there [by virtue of her having accommodation available to her, perhaps] or resident there in fact [because she lives in the UK] you must either leave her name off the application form and have the account in your name only, or be prepared to have income tax deducted from all the interest.

Building societies and banks apart where else might you put your excess earnings? Where should you look to "invest" rather than "save" your money?

Nowhere, unless you know what you are doing and why you are doing it.

To many new expatriates "investment" may be a word that they will have understood but, due to lack of capital, never uttered. **Investment is the accumulation of monies in an open-ended commitment with the hope of gain.** In basics nothing more than that. With proper professional advice it is hard enough to read the writing on the walls of the world's stock exchanges; probably nigh on impossible if you are none too sure whether the *Commersbank-Gesamtindex* is a hock of dubious parentage or the index against which West German stocks and shares are measured.

For many expatriates the period of service abroad lasts only a few years. Such a relatively short time in which to accumulate capital necessitates the following of a carefully thought out investment plan. And the first ingredient of that plan should almost always be a question; something like "why am I doing this?" Allied to "why aren't I spending all this cash to-day rather than investing it to spend in the future?"

Answer those two questions and in the unlikely event that you can, after serious thought, think of no eventuality or ambition for which you ought be investing then spend the money. That is what money is for.

More often than not you will have an answer; you will have an objective and have an idea of the time span over which you intend to have that objective more clearly in your sights.

It may be that in three years time you want to buy a house rather than live in rented accommodation. You realise, no doubt, that you will require a mortgage but feel that you ought do something to ensure that you have a large deposit. Perhaps in eighteen months time you would like to pay off your existing mortgage and feel that you have achieved a substantial objective. Or you might want sufficient capital in two years time to go into business on your own account rather than work for someone else. Do you want, passionately, to buy a Porsche 928S at the end of next year?

If you have any of those objectives then investment is not for you! You should be putting your money directly into a building society or bank account.

Investment inevitably involves slow, steady growth over a period of years longer than one or two; it is true that often investment media [stocks and shares, unit or managed funds] will outstrip bank or building society interest over such a brief period. But they cannot guarantee to do so; and if the Porsche is so important or the ideal of owning your own home so high on your list of priorities then you need a little more of guarantees and somewhat less of "maybe".

However, where investment can really come into play is where, in answer to your self questioning, you come up with objectives such as investing to-day and to-morrow to reap rewards five or ten years ahead. You may see the necessity to fund to-day for pension planning fifteen or twenty years hence. You may if you are wise; in which case investing now, whilst you are an expatriate, and reaping the rewards when you are not will be a short term funding for a long term project. Here some types of investment come into their own. **Some types of investment only!**

I personally do not include in that category fine wines, fine carpets, fine jewellery or fine art; nor investment stamps or commodities such as copper, coffee or tea. There is, undoubtedly a place for such investments in the overall portfolio of many people; but they need to be already wealthy, well-advised and capable of standing losses as well as recognising when they can make a "killing" and flee the market.

Neither would I actively encourage most expatriates to start investing in property other than for their own or a dependent's occupation. The up-front costs of buying and furnishing houses are very high. Wherever you live in the world the rental income from UK property is always assessable for tax [see the chapter devoted to the UK Home] and, unless you or a dependent relative is occupying it, capital gains tax is payable if you sell whilst resident in the UK.

No! The type of investment that inevitably can be tailored to suit a personal requirement is either a **unit trust, a managed fund off-shore of the UK,** [or a portfolio of both allied with direct investment into stock markets which you either manage yourself or pay someone else to do so for you.]

Before becoming an expatriate it is quite likely that you will have had little or no need for an understanding of what a "unit trust" is or how it works. Now, with more investment muscle and more money with which to flex it you might be somewhat uncertain of how fund managers work.

Any caring adviser will understand your lack of knowledge; any fund manager will be happy to explain the ramifications of his investment plans and the way they work so I do not intend to spend a great deal of time dealing with the intricacies here. It is, however, important that you recognise the role that "unitised" investment plans can play in your financial well-being and the overall concept of this particular investment market.

The basic idea behind the unit trust and managed fund markets is quite simple. Professional management of that part of your capital or investment income directed at the world's stock markets serves two major functions. Firstly it reduces the "risk factor" by adding expert knowledge to the spreading of the risks which are involved in any investment and also relieves you, as the investor, from day to day administration of your portfolio.

Any unitised fund is, basically, one in which the money under the managers' control is divided into equal parts or units. Each unit represents an interest in the overall monies under management; the value of that interest is determined by the number of units issued. If the holdings of the fund are worth £50,000,000 and there are 25,000,000 units issued then the value of each unit will be £2.00.

This price does not, contrary to popular belief, rise or fall because someone else buys or sells his units; the fluctuations in price occur only when the underlying market value of the fund increases or diminishes. When the fund manager takes in more cash for investment he buys more securities; the number of units rises in proportion to the money under management. If an investor wants to encash his holding of units then the manager sells securities to cover the repayment and thus the status quo of units to fund value is maintained.

Off-shore funds — advertised as particularly relevant to expatriates since they are not subjected to the rigours of UK taxation — differ very slightly in concept to the

authorised unit trusts in the UK. They tend, for example, to issue "shares" rather than "units"; they have wider investment opportunities than those imposed upon their UK counterparts by the regulatory authorities in the UK.

Daily "dealing" prices are rare in these off-shore funds; commonplace in authorised unit trusts in the UK. The offshore funds are often denominated in currencies other than sterling.

This lack of UK control over the off-shore fund managers activities should not be seen as any deterrent to investing in them. Most off-shore financial centres [such as the Channel Islands] impose their own strictly observed regulations on the fund managers working within their shores. Choose the right fund manager, located in the right low tax area and investing with an eye on the sort of results you wish to achieve and you will not go far wrong.

Without the assistance of either any financial adviser or stockbroker many expatriate investors manage their affairs so well that they consistently beat indices by which stock market performance [and hence unit trust performance, indirectly] is measured.

Quite how or quite why some investors are so fortunate is often a mystery; a mystery which is perhaps best not explored other than to remark that "gut" instinct is a valuable asset when it is right and a "pain in the pinny" when it is wrong. Generally, though, most expatriates leave the management of their invested monies either directly in the hands of the fund managers or to their investment adviser, be he a stockbroker or a financial specialist of another hue. Often they are wise to do so.

They may have been used to dealing direct with modest investments whilst they were in the UK; have grown used to tax impositions upon gains and ACT on dividends. Dealing with an internationally spread portfolio is best left to the experts.

The interaction of taxes in the country in which the shares of the company are registered with the taxes imposed in the expatriate's country of residence can be very complicated; country "A" may impose a withholding tax on dividends of ordinary shares quoted on its stock market whilst allowing the "income" from fixed interest, government-backed securities to be paid gross. Country "B" may reverse the situation and impose withholding tax, subsequently recoverable under a tax treaty — or totally irrecoverable — on both or neither.

Simplicity with dependability should be the expatriate's primary aim.

Ideally the headaches of investment management should be left to the experts; a painless and often tax efficient way of achieving this idea is through the better of the managed funds specifically designed to help achieve that aim.

Many fund managers will accept discretion from clients investing with them and manage portfolios in an attempt to achieve the specific, pre-advised aims of that client.

Specialist firms of financial advisers will do the same; often with more verve

than the "in house" managers can be expected to show. The independent adviser will have the entire palette of funds from which to design his client's future; the fund manager might feel more inclined to manage a portfolio of his own funds rather than invest too heavily with competitors.

Remember also the one cardinal rule of investment summed up for me a few months ago by an old friend of mine who is a stockbroker with a rare commodity for his breed; a sense of houmour. "Any silly * * * * er can buy into an investment market" he declared "its the silly * * * that expects me to know exactly when to get out that scares the * * * * out of me most of the time".

More often than not, with sound advice, a little luck in choosing the right investment and the ability not to panic when a unit or a share falls in value by ten per cent, many investors can make substantial profits over a medium to long term.

Some advisers, and indeed some fund managers, are what might be called "market backers" whilst others could be described as "share pickers".

Those who primarily study and try to predict the performance of a particular stock market [or set of stock markets] tend to do so with an eye on the economic trends in the country or area of the world under their scrutiny. They tend, if their choice is right, to produce steady growth in the investments under their care.

Those who expertly study the individual stocks which help to comprise any particular stock market and invest in them, rather than taking a more overall view of the performance of the index of the market, can make heftier profits since their particular choice of share could rise dramatically whilst other shares are just "so so". However, it has to be said that if the choice is not wise the investment can also fail more dramatically too.

As I say, these are decisions upon which it is wise to take professional advice.

Discussion between you and your adviser is of paramount importance; he must know your philosophy and you must get an inkling of how he proposes to assist you achieve your financial objectives.

Many expatriates are slack about giving their advisers facts which would help the adviser assess personal philosophy and ambitions for the money being invested and then, when objectives are not achieved, they moan long and hard. The adviser takes the blame; not willingly but he takes it all the same.

Apart from the initial discussions — which as I have indicated should be in-depth discussions — you should also ensure regular "check-up" sessions. Home leave is obviously the time for these extra discussions with your advisers; but please do them the courtesy of making an appointment. Too often expatriates leave everything in this respect to the last minute and then expect the adviser to be available at a moment's notice; fitted in between fond farewell parties with their mates and the departure time of the aircraft.

The same courtesy should be extended to bank managers and society managers. Pleased as most of them always are to meet expatriate customers and members to discuss financial affairs they are always even more pleased when they have been given sufficient notice to prepare themselves, especially if they have to take advice from colleagues dealing in specific areas of your accounts with them.

Bank managers, some building society managers and investment advisers [particularly investment advisers] make up a much maligned community. Such a reputation is, in a few instances, richly deserved. However the greatest dis-satisfaction with the financial institutions comes from those expatriates who expect miracles from mortals. One eminent financial journalist summed up the situation in one sentence. "Doctors" he said "bury their mistakes; financial advisers have to live with theirs".

You will be giving your financial adviser, whether he be accountant, banker, building society manager, investment adviser or stockbroker more of a chance to live happily with you if you are prepared to be specific in your requirements, prepared to give him an insight into your personal philosophy and, above all, prepared to allow him to alter your way of thinking. Never present your adviser, of whatever professional persuasion, with preconceived plans which have only a predestined ending.

The investment and savings ploys available to you as an expatriate allow you to be flexible in your approach to your financial aims. Take advantage of all the specialist knowledge that is readily available to you.

INSURANCE

The ethics of some insurance salesmen come under severe criticism from time to time; much of it is unwarranted and fanned by ill-informed comment in the media.

In this chapter I shall explore but a few of the essential products and services of insurance industry; or at least those sections of it which provide protection or savings plans which many of us need rather than feel that we want.

Life insurance and assurance policies

I hate ever having to be involved in choosing wall-paper or curtain materials. The myriad patterns and designs confuse me so, unless I fairly soon find something that appeals or there is a persistent salesman there to help me make up my mind, I walk out of the shop after a preliminary skirmish.

That is no real way to tackle the problem of choice because it only means that I delay the evil day and have to return to begin the hassles again. I sometimes wish there were only two patterns to choose from; it would make everything so much easier.

Fortunately there **are** only two types of life policies and once you have grasped the essential differences it makes it so much easier to choose the type that suits your circumstances.

All life policies are insurance or assurance or made up of a mixture of both; I am afraid that despite the life assurance industry's attempts to complicate the whole affair, life policies are as simple as that.

Life insurance is the easiest to explain and, for the family man, the type of cover most essential to his needs.

We insure ourselves against a risk that might happen to us or to our property. We insure ourselves against having to pay private medical expenses or against dying at a time when our death would place a particular financial burden on our family. We insure our cars and our homes against accidental damage, theft or fire.

Insurance is always used to describe a type of policy which covers us against something that we hope will not happen but which might happen.

Assurance — there is only one type of policy issued which is assurance and that is life assurance it indicates that we are providing for an event we know, one day, will happen. You are going to die one day; so am I. To cover the financial loss to our families on the happening of that event we need life assurance; we do not know when we are going to die, just that we will; not "might" but "will".

The life companies have so many statistics at their finger-tips that they reckon that they can assess for example when an averagely healthy man of 25 following an averagely risky occupation might die. Not for them "give or take ten years" but [remember it is only a statistical prediction] to an accuracy of two places of decimals; he has 48.59 years ahead of him. If he is suffering from a mild but chronic disease his life span [delicately called his "expectancy"] will be lessened by a year or so.

An averagely fit man of 58 might expect to live another 19.05 years; giving him an overall expected life span around 3.56 years longer than his 25 year old son! If you want to argue the logic of that statement blame statistics, not me.

It is upon these statistics that life companies can calculate the premiums they will charge to assure or insure our lives. The statistics also show that a woman of your age or mine will live [on average] four years longer than we will; statistics say so.

Therefore premiums for women are calculated on the assumption that she is a male life four years younger than she actually is.

I do not, I have to say, generally find statistics anything other than boring but the actuarial statistics used by life companies do serve a useful purpose or two; not only can they indicate the right premium for a life company to charge but they categorically prove that we are all going to die one day.

Having accepted that we have to ask ourselves who will suffer financially if we die before statistics say we will or if, sticking strictly to the calculations, we die on the predicted day.

Having come to a conclusion our next step is to work out whether our financial commitment to others is best covered by insurance or assurance.

Cost might dictate our choice; because **insurance** is against a "maybe" and **assurance** is planning for a "will be" insurance is cheaper than assurance.

Gordon Green is 35 years old and works in Saudi Arabia; unable to join him because she is looking after two small children [Grace, aged three and Greg, aged six] Gladys Green, his wife, is back in the UK. Gordon is provided with some accident insurance by his employers but has no life policies. The accident cover provides Gladys and the children with some financial recompense only if Gordon dies of anything other than natural causes. So let us suggest what role life policies can play.

Who will suffer most if Gordon dies before his statistically calculated life span says he will?

Gladys, Grace and Greg will.

During what period are Gordon's family particularly at risk?

From to-day through to when Grace leaves school and gets a job and can start to support herself. That is in fifteen years time so what we need to suggest to Gordon is that he would be as well insuring his life for a fifteen year period so that were he to die during that time his family would be financially secure.

Would Gladys prefer a lump sum of money on Gordon's premature death or would she prefer a tax free income upon which she can raise the children, run the house and buy the necessities of life?

Statistics show that Gladys will prefer the second with the option to change her mind and take the first. I refrain from adding the obvious remark since I have appeared to be unkind to women in the tax chapter.

Can the life companies cope with this need?

Yes, they can, quite easily and quite inexpensively with a policy generally known as Family Income Benefit; all Gordon and Gladys have to decide is the size of the income upon which she would be able to live were she to be without Gordon's financial support whilst the children were on-hand. The choice is theirs but shall we suggest that £10,000 per annum, tax free, would be a reasonable choice? Taking into consideration too that they will want to keep the premiums at an affordable level;

particularly if Gordon returns to the UK and has to pay the premiums out of a lower, taxed UK income.

In essence Gordon will arrange with the life company that they insure his life for 15 years for an initial sum insured today of £150,000 which will reduce every year he lives of the 15 years by £10,000.

If he dies at the end of the first year [from what ever cause] the insurance company will pay Gladys £10,000 a year, tax free, for the remaining fourteen years of the policy. Or she may decide [on advice from her bank manager or solicitor] to ask the insurance company for a commuted lump sum instead of the annual income. She has the choice and need not think about exercising it unless Gordon dies before Grace is eighteen years old. We have not overlooked Greg. He is still a factor in calculating the amount of cover Gordon needs to provide but he will be out from under the "umbrella" of protection the policy provides three years before Grace leaves school.

An initial sum insured of £150,000 is a lot of money but because the sum insured reduces by £10,000 each year and because the life company can assess Gordon's chances of surviving the 15 year period [after a medical examination, no doubt] the premium he has to pay is modest; around £10 a month. A great deal of sum insured for a minimal, affordable premium.

The premiums are so low because statistics tell the life company that Gordon is unlikely to die within the fifteen year period. The life company can afford to take the risk: but can Gordon — or rather his family — make such an assumption? Can they, for so small an outlay, take the risk when the consequences of them being wrong would be so financially disastrous?

But what if the statistics are right? What if he lives the 15 year period and sees Grace leave school and go to university or to work. What will he get out of the policy?

Nothing, other than the knowledge that he covered a risk that might have happened. He will have spent, over the years, about £1,800 and received nothing but protection for his family. He bought an "umbrella" and it did not rain.

That is a risk that he took and he might selfishly look back on the expenditure and convince himself that it was not worth it.

But the peace of mind was worth it and remember that, unlike other "umbrella" shops, life companies are none too keen to sell people like Gordon the protection his family need to shelter under once it has started "raining".

There are many other forms of life insurance; all designed to provide money [income or capital] on the death of the life insured.

There are also many needs for the protection which life insurance provides; covering perhaps the repayment of an outstanding mortgage, a debt to a bank or a friend, the possibility that a parent might die before a liability to pay school fees is completed, a need to provide for the payment of UK inheritance tax on a gift inter vivos.

There is also a form of life insurance, generally known as "convertible term" insurance which allows the life insured to enjoy the benefit of the protection which the policy provides whilst giving him an inalienable right [over a period of five or ten years, say] to change the whole or part of the sum insured into endowment, whole of life policies or further term insurance.

Since I have not yet discussed such endowment or whole life policies I shall revert to the very important options contained in convertible term insurance a little later in the chapter.

This chapter is not intended as an unpaid advertisement for the life insurance industry but so important a form of life cover cannot [or, at least, should not] be dismissed in a few paragraphs. So I shall delve a little deeper into the possible needs which Gordon, or you, might have for the protection which these policies provide.

The one thing I am loth to do is to pre-empt your seeking professional advice; take advice from a specialist adviser well-versed in the field of insurance policies and who, with your personal circumstances at his finger tips, will be able to design a melange of policies tailored to your individual needs. Please, therefore take everything I say on the subject as generalisations, even if, perchance, I describe in my examples situations which apply very roughly to you.

Please do not be tempted into any short cuts.

What you require to do is to consult a professional specialist in life insurance matters and to discuss with him [or her; there are many fine women life insurance advisers in practice] the "made to measure" schemes that are available.

Apart from convertible term, to which I shall revert later, there are, as I say, a number of covers provided by life insurance policies which might relieve you of a worry and your family of a huge financial headache should you die before any particular financial commitment expires.

Many expatriates whom I have met have suggested that they would buy more life policies if only they could understand the ramifications.

That is not a reason; it is a silly excuse.

If you are bothered about the somewhat tortuous language in which life policies are necessarily couched [and in which some advisers on life insurance unnecessarily speak] then dismiss your fears. You should not be pedantic enough to feel that you need be fully aware of all the nuances of every contractual document you enter into: were that the case you would never go on an airplane. Have you ever sat down and read the exclusions printed in very small print on your tickets?

Family Income Benefit

I have already touched on the sort of protection FIB can provide. It is term insurance; reducing term insurance at that. The initial sum insured reduces by level amounts each year the life insured lives; then, if he expires before the policy expires, what is still left in the "kitty" is paid out in instalments, usually monthly or quarterly, for the remainder of the policy's life.

It is often quite difficult for someone who sees the sense of effecting FIB to come to any logical conclusion as to what level of benefit he ought insure for. After all, not only does he need to take account of any inflationary tendencies but also the amount of premium which he can happily afford. Expatriates can usually afford quite high premiums to-day but what of tomorrow, next week or next year?

If you have committed yourself to paying several hundred pounds a year to-day you have, surely, to be convinced that when you return to the UK you will be able to go on affording the premiums.

Arriving at the length of time for which the possible benefit should be insured can be a little easier; very much easier if you know already that no more little Johnnies or Belindas are going to arrive and spoil your plans.

Say you have two children aged four and six years old and let us say that either Nature or you have determined that you will leave it at that. You will know that your real vulnerability period, the length of time when FIB will really be needed is, at a minimum, fourteen years. That will see your younger child leaving school, shaving, going out with boys [or all three!]

Your elder child will arrive at eighteen two years earlier and so will be able to leave the protection of the umbrella FIB provides before the younger child. So the length of time the cover should run can, in this circumstance, be fairly accurately calculated.

But what if you are not finished [or not even started] having children. Then what?

In such cases there is but one scientifically proven aid to calculating the amount of benefit and the length of time the policy will have to run.

It is known as having a guess.

A guess based on a bit of common sense, like all good guesses are.

I shall assume that you are somewhere between twenty five and thirty five, have been married a year or two with plans to have a family. Plans, in this respect, can sadly go astray but common sense would dictate that around the age of forty you will either have had all the children you want or you will have had none at all.

What you should do, now, is effect Family Income Benefit for twenty or twenty five years. By and large that will cover your vulnerability period since within that time your family will be determined and half grown up.

What you should not do is await the first signs of the children arriving. You may not be fit; life insurance may not be obtainable and then with a family started and no way of getting the cover you require. Just as important, as I shall explain, your wife, now pregnant, will be unlikely to be quite so desirable a life insurance prospect. She will have to wait until the baby is born before she can propose to a life insurance company for cover on her life.

I have tabulated below average monthly premiums for male lives [in averagely good health] to provide £100 per annum FIB cover [over 10, 15, 20 and 25 years] for ages 25, 30 and 35. See how reasonable the premiums are, use a little common sense in determining the level of benefit required and do something about it NOW!

FAMILY INCOME BENEFIT
Monthly premiums to secure £100 p.a. benefit

Male aged	25 years £	30 years £	35 years £
Benefit years			
10	0.052	0.052	0.060
15	0.060	0.078	0.104
20	0.086	0.112	0.155
25	0.112	0.165	0.224

So, a man aged thirty wishing to effect FIB for £10,000 per annum for 25 years would pay a monthly premium of £16.50. An initial sum insured of a quarter of a million pounds for a monthly outlay of £16.50!

Earlier I indicated that no wife should wait until she is pregnant to effect cover on her own life.

I am not in any way suggesting that life insurance companies regard pregnant women as being "unwell" but, safe as modern obstetric methods are, patently a pregnant woman is more at risk while she is pregnant than before. I am, however, suggesting that a wife and mother is a very valuable member of the family; valuable in the financial sense as well as any other. Therefore she too ought be covered by Family Income Benefit. The premiums will be cheaper than those on your life since she is regarded as being four years younger than she actually is.

Other term insurances

Practically all of us have a mortgage; if it is a straight forward repayment mortgage with a building society it may be that we need **Mortgage Protection** insurance to repay the outstanding loan and accrued interest in the event that we die before the mortgage is paid off.

We may be indebted to a bank or a member of our family for a loan they have made us; again life insurance can provide essential cover, making sure that if we die before the loan is repaid the policy proceeds rather than our estate will bear the brunt of the debt.

Any of us may receive a gift of money from parents or other elderly relatives. If, having made us the gift, the donor was to die within seven years then a liability to inheritance tax will arise as I have explained in the tax chapter. The insurance industry can provide reducing term insurance cover which we can effect on the life of the donor; thus any liability to inheritance tax can be taken into account. This form of reducing term insurance is known as ***"gift inter vivos"*** insurance.

If you need the benefit of any of these covers then the person to have discussions with is your insurance adviser.

Such discussion with a professional specialist might also reveal the need for life

assurance. Hardly ever, in discussions with a caring professional, will a couple with a family ever hear the word "assurance" before the adviser has explored the clients' needs for "insurance". Regrettably, due to the way that commission on life policies is structured, few salesmen who visit the expatriate areas of the world ever let the word "insurance" pass their lips.

Commission on "insurance" policies is considerably less than it is on some "assurance" policies [where commission can range up to 45% of the first year's premium and beyond.] Life insurance premiums are what is known amongst the life companies as "thin"; another way of saying, presumably, that there isn't much fat on them for the salesman to get in commission.

So what role can life assurance policies play in anyone's overall financial strategy?

The two main, conventional life assurance policies are **endowment assurances** and **whole of life assurances;** they may participate in the profits of the assurance company or be a straight "non-profit" contract. They may also be tied to the performance of a unit trust or a mixture of unit trusts. The latter type being a relatively modern innovation in the long history of the life assurance industry.

It is also the type of policy which may have grown into disrepute amongst some sections of the expatriate community due to the enthusiasm with which many salesmen have encouraged expatriates to buy an excess number of them. A rather long-winded way of saying what I would have preferred to say; that is **too many salesmen have flogged this type of policy to anyone and everyone without a great deal of professionalism being involved.** But I will refrain from putting it that way for fear I might upset some salesmen's sensibilities; they can get a mite touchy.

Whole of life policies, as the name suggests, pay benefits upon the death of the life assured; a very simple arrangement. You love your family dearly and want them to have financial support at your death when ever it occurs; tomorrow or in fifty years time. With profit, without profit or linked to the performance of unit trusts in some way. You can make your choice according to your feelings in the matter. I know what my feelings are but you choose the last one if you want to.

I have left until now any detailed comment about **"convertible term"** insurance; as I explained earlier, until I had dealt with the two major life assurance policies, I felt it advisable to leave convertible term alone.

That is not what you should do; convertible term is almost as essential a cover for the family man as is Family Income Benefit.

Convertible term insurance, as its name suggests, is ordinary term insurance with built in conversion options.

Let us say that, having decided that you need FIB [and we have decided that, haven't we?] you remain undecided about the need for life assurance policies. You can see some reason for having endowment or whole of life assurance but cannot decide that now is the moment to effect the policies.

Convertible term provides the answer. For a few pounds a month you can secure the benefits of extra life insurance cover for, say, a 5 or 10 year period knowing that at any time during that period you can, whatever the state of your health, convert the whole or part of the sum insured to endowment or whole of life policies.

Note please that I said that you "can" convert the convertible term; there is no in-built guarantee on your part that you "will". The life company is the party to this bargain who is giving the guarantees; it is guaranteeing to accept you for endowment or whole of life policies up to the sum insured.

So, if you are undecided about life assurance policies, go half way and effect convertible term insurance. Once again I have shown you some convertible term rates; since anyone of any age can be undecided I have extended the table of premiums from the age of 25 right through to the age of 55. I have taken 10, 15 and 20 years as the initial term of the insurance; the term can be adjusted to suit your personal requirements. Discuss the matter with your insurance adviser.

CONVERTIBLE TERM INSURANCE

monthly premiums to secure sum insured £10,000

Male Aged	**25**	**30**	**35**	**40**	**45**	**50**
Years of cover	**£**	**£**	**£**	**£**	**£**	**£**
10	**1.90**	**1.22**	**1.57**	**2.79**	**4.82**	**8.05**
15	**1.10**	**1.43**	**1.98**	**3.60**	**6.24**	**10.23**
20	**1.24**	**1.70**	**2.67**	**4.76**	**7.89**	**n/a**

So a man aged thirty could effect £100,000 convertible term cover on his life for a 20 year period for just £12.40 a month. A huge amount of cover should he die within the period and all the time in the world to make up his mind about his future life assurance needs as they arise.

How can you ensure that the benefits from any policy at your death actually end up in the hands of the person or persons you wish to receive them?

If you simply take out any form of insurance or assurance policy without taking a little time or making a little effort to understand what might at first sight seem a complexity then, almost without doubt the person or persons whom you would wish to benefit as soon after your death as possible will have to wait for the benefits to pass through the hands of your executors; assuming always that you have made a will and the person or persons are amongst the beneficiaries. And assuming always that some large creditor does not get to your estate first.

Life policies "in trust"

You can ensure the speedy, uncomplicated movement of the policy monies from the life company to your chosen beneficiaries at your death, with full protection from any creditors, by arranging [at the time you effect the policy] that the life company issues the policy "under trust" naming the persons you wish to benefit as the beneficiaries. The complexities are minimal, the cost of writing the policy "under trust" is often as low as nothing, and you will have the added comfort of knowing that the whole essence of life policies taken out for the benefit of others will be intact; money in the right hands at the right time.

Any life company will be pleased to arrange the necessary simple trust documents for you; any caring professional life assurance adviser will explain the procedure and the structure of writing the policy under trust. Please listen to what you are advised to do and if the result seems to be in accord with your wishes then do it.

Endowment assurance polices may also be written under trust; but since endowment policies are essentially savings plans with some death cover knitting the savings portions together and since writing a policy under trust in reality gives the benefit of the policy monies to someone else, you may prefer to leave the contracts on what is known as "own life, own benefit" basis. You will have no difficulty in collecting the proceeds of the policy in person if you survive to the maturity date of the policy.

If you die before the envisaged maturity of the policy the proceeds will pass into the hands of your executors to be distributed, along with the rest of your estate, according to the dictates of your will.

There is a method, [sounds complex but is not] whereby endowment policies can be written under trust in such a way that if you die the benefit goes to beneficiaries; if you live to see the maturity of the policy the benefit reverts to you. Well worth exploring with your insurance adviser; it is known as writing the policy in trust on a "reverter to disponer" basis. Even I have to get into the complex descriptions sometimes!

Life of another

One other way exists to ensure the speedy payment of benefits under life insurance and assurance contracts on the death of the life covered by the policy.

If someone can establish what is known as an "insurable interest" in your life then he or she may — but only with your permission and co-operation — effect a policy on your life and be paid the benefits of the policy proceeds if you die within the contractural period of the policy. In the case of an endowment policy, were you to live to the maturity date, the proceeds would be paid to the person assuring your life; technically he or she is known as the "grantee" of the policy.

Under English law everyone has unlimited insurable interest in his own life or in the life of his wife; likewise she has unlimited insurable interest in her husband's life.

So, instead of writing policies under trust, you and your wife might see the good sense in insuring one another. Each of you will own the policy for which you pay the premiums; all the other is doing is providing a sort of fleshy coat hanger upon which the policy is draped. If either of you dies within the contract period then the other collects the policy proceeds simply by proving the event to the life company and presenting them with the policy. No waiting for probate; another way of ensuring money in the right hands at the right time.

Under English law no-one else, other than you and your wife, has automatic insurable interest in your life. In Scotland the rules are very slightly different and provide that in some circumstances parents have insurable interest in the lives of their children and vice versa.

But other insurable interests can be established.

If, for example, I loaned you £10,000 for a five year period I might consider it a very wise move to insure your life for £10,000. Hard hearted as I might be I would not want to think that were you to die before paying me back I would have to badger your widow and children for the money. So — again I repeat, with your permission and co-operation — I could go to the life company and effect five year term insurance on your life and, were you to die before paying me back, collect the proceeds instead. I will have established what is known as a "pecuniary" interest in you. And how!

A quirk of insurance law is that the insurable interest I have established has only to exist at the time the policy is effected.

If shortly after taking the loan from me you win the pools and pay me back the cash you borrowed I can, if I wish, continue the policy. If you die within the five years I collect again. Indeed, there is nothing to stop me, in the first instance, effecting whole of life endowment assurance upon your life; I need not limit the period of the policy to coincide with the time I expect you to pay me back.

When you die I will collect the money without any liability to income tax, capital gains tax or inheritance tax.

I am not, I assure you, likely to lend you £10,000; you do not need it anyway, being a rich working British expatriate. So how about you making me a substantial gift? Send me £50000 and I will go away and not bother you any more.

But wait! Before I go, there might be the little matter of inheritance tax for me to worry about. I explained in the tax chapter that if you die within seven years of making me the gift there will be an inheritance tax liability and you will not want to suffer that too, will you?

I shall have established an insurable interest to the amount of the tax liability and — with your permission and co-operation — would be wise to cover the risk by insuring your life.

Or what about if we were to go into business together; we would surely worry about the fact that one of us could die at a crucial time in our business relationship.

We would have a pecuniary interest in one another and need to insure the risk involved.

I have made plain that we could only do so with one another's permission and co-operation. Often, in TV or filmed drama, we see young and beautiful wives seducing young and vulnerable insurance salesmen into issuing policies on the life of the soon-to-be-defunct husband then arranging a convenient accident; usually by sawing through a brake cable on the car.

It cannot be done; saw away as long as you wish ladies but you will not get any British life company to issue a policy on your husband's life without he signs the proposal form and indicates that he is permitting you to effect the insurance.

Sorry if, yet again, I have disturbed anyone's plans for their future financial well-being.

Joint life policies

There was once a vogue — now, thankfully, largely passed — for insuring or assuring the lives of husband and wife under one policy. It was arranged that on the death of the first to die the benefit was paid; this left the survivor without any cover but that seemed rarely to occur to anyone. It was also possible for the benefit to be paid on the death of the second person covered under the policy; it still is for that matter. In some very specific circumstances there is a need for joint life insurance or assurance policies but only in specific circumstances and only on the advice of a competent life assurance counsellor.

Do not be persuaded by a friend or a colleague that the idea of joint lives policies applies to you simply because in a moment of weakness, or on the occasion of a specific need, he effected policies in this way.

Foreign currency insurance and assurance

There was also a period during which insurance and assurance policies in foreign currencies were very much in vogue. They are still available and in some instances serve an important — even essential — purpose but, in general, it is unwise [for the same reasons as it is unwise to have too great an exposure to currency risks in bank accounts] to consider foreign currency policies as being an ingredient of most expatriates' portfolio of policies.

It must be remembered that the premiums of the policies must be paid for in the currency in which the benefits are denominated; Swiss francs must be paid to secure Swiss francs on death or maturity of the policy. Long term insurance and assurance policies may both demand the continuation of foreign currency premiums once you have returned to the UK. Exchange risk exposure in both paying the premiums and receiving the benefits must be taken into account.

The major role of foreign currency policies is in the provision of cover for a foreign currency debt; perhaps you have started to buy a property in Spain or France and will be repaying a loan or will wish to discharge a liability in pesetas or francs in the event of your death before payment for the property is completed.

Please remember that the essential role of insurance and assurance policies is to provide the right money in the right hands at the right time. In this context "right money" should be taken also to mean "right currency". British milkmen and building societies, rating officers and odd-job men like to be paid for their services in the coin of Her Majesty's realm. None will happily wait to be paid simply because your widow is left with the problem of wondering whether she ought to pay their demands immediately or wait until the exchange rate between sterling and Swiss francs is ideal.

Unit linked assurance

Many authorised unit trusts [in the UK] or off-shore managed funds [outside the UK] have arrangements with life companies whereby the "investment" section of life assurance policies is tied to the performance of the funds under management. Instead of the policy holders' assurance plan participating in the profits accrued within the life fund of the assurance company it is geared to the profits which the unit trust or managed fund produces.

One of the reasons that many people effect unit-linked life assurance policies is that when the proceeds are taken from the policy they benefit from advantageous tax treatment enjoyed by life assurance policy holders. But against the personal tax advantages has to be balanced the fact that within the life fund income received and capital gains made are taxable.

Similar policies issued by off-shore companies will not normally be subjected to these tax disadvantages; such policies effected before the UK Finance Act 1984 had even more in their favour. But now, since the 1984 strictures, it is necessary to preserve the off-shore tax advantages by substituting the policy for a UK based policy when the expatriate policy holder returns to the UK to resume tax residence.

All the major off-shore life companies have perfected this "switching" procedure so this hiccup ought to be only a minor detraction from their use in the right circumstances.

What has to be considered, and considered carefully, is just what those right circumstances are; obviously individual circumstances will be different and it will be up to you, in consultation with your adviser, to determine whether such off-shore insurance policies have any place in your investment portfolio. You must weigh everything very carefully.

On the one hand there are the tax advantages; on the other might be your reluctance to "lock" into one investment manager's skills a considerable amount of money each year for a minimum of ten years.

There can be little doubt that assurance policies have a part to play in many expatriates' plans for the future; whether the policies be endowments to assist with savings for retirement or whole of life policies to fund for financial support for dependents at the policy holder's death.

There can also be little doubt that, due largely to the commission structure, life

assurance is in danger of being over-sold when life insurance [in one of its guises] would be more suitable.

Provided you are aware of that and choose both your adviser and the policies carefully, and have due regard for the fact that many policies will demand substantial premiums from you for a considerable number of years, the life companies have many products which warrant your attention.

Health Insurances

Whereas we all accept that we are going to die at some time, too few of us ever consider the high risks we run of requiring private medical attention and the cost of private hospitalisation.

Neither do we happily foresee the day when illness or disability might prevent us earning a living. Whilst we are fit and whilst we are busy working — and generally enjoying both — we tend to push such thoughts into the background.

But if we can take time to consider the financial consequences of acute medical conditions or long term illnesses we shall find that the cost to our financial well-being is considerable and that the insurance companies issue policies which cover all the eventualities of which we should be aware.

There are a number of companies who have developed "international" schemes to provide hospitalisation and medical cover; some include the expenses of emergency repatriation from anywhere in the world to the UK in the event that treatment would seem to be required at home by a specialist surrounded by the right facilities.

Continuing in reasonably good health is something we all tend to take for granted; with the help of a general practitioner [albeit, in many countries the cost of his advice can be considerable] most of us remain fairly fit. It is when we are involved in the unwanted and unexpected medical emergency that the truth that we are "human" hits us.

Particularly so if we are being paid a substantial amount of money to do what ever we do; the shortest time we are away from work and the more complete our recovery the better it will be for us.

The biggest and most pertinent investment we ever make is ensuring that we are fit to earn a living; all other regular savings or investments we might make rely upon us to feed them with money.

Medical and hospitalisation insurances are two of the ways in which the prudent man ensures that the high costs of private treatment are borne with some equanimity.

Permanent Health Insurance

An odd title for an essential cover. Permanent Health Insurance [PHI as it is generally known] does not guarantee us continued good health but insures us against the risks of becoming ill or disabled and, as a result, having to face a considerable drop in our earning capacity.

You might think that prolonged illness is a fairly remote possibility and that as long as you have provided for your family in the event of your death they are sufficiently well protected.

But long term inability to work as a result of an accident or serious illness is a far more common misfortune than people generally realise.

Statistics compiled by the UK Social Security Department show that one in six men in the UK will be off work for at least six months before he retires, and that a considerable number of them will never be fit enough to return to work again.

Comparable statistics do not exist for expatriate British workers; it must be pretty self-evident that if they did they would show that at best the figures were similar: more likely worse due to climatic and other "conditions".

That is where PHI can help; by providing a replacement income should you be unfortunate enough to be off work for a considerable time, no matter what caused the disability or whether you are living in the UK or abroad.

PHI is designed to start paying benefit after you have been too ill to work for a certain length of time — 13 or 26 weeks is the norm.

This deferred period ensures that financial support is provided when you need it most — once the bills start piling up and other sources of income have dried up. PHI then provides financial support until you are able to return to work. Benefit is not discontinued if you remain too unwell to work more than a certain length of time and you do not have to be hospitalised to claim.

Specific details as to the amount of benefits available and the premiums required to secure them differ from company to company; you should enquire [or, even better, your adviser should know] which company's product suits your circumstances best.

Choosing an insurer

No insurance company is best at everything; were that so there would only be one insurance company. And in Britain alone there are two or three hundred.

You could spend a frustrating year and a half writing to all of them and reading the sales literature they will willingly send you; you would still not have made a choice. And in that time you could have died; or become ill or disabled and uninsurable. If you have none of the insurances that I suggested that you need you have to make the decision to get cover **now**; not in eighteen months time.

Being an expatriate does not make it any easier to choose.

Whereas some insurance companies have set their sights firmly on encouraging expatriate policy holders there are a few life assurance offices [especially] who appear still to live in the first half of the nineteenth century and who abhor the idea of anyone living or working south of the Isle of Wight proposing to them for life policies.

The firms who advertise their plans for expatriates — whether they be savings plans, protection plans or those providing the cover of medical, hospitalisation or permanent health insurance — are obviously keen to attract you.

It is also very likely that they have designed plans which recognise that you are not living within the UK and which are more likely to cover the needs or provide the savings plans which might attract you. So try them first. It will save you a lot of time; and time in insurance matters is, as I have tried to impress upon you, all important.

Most family men of between 30 and 45 years of age, with the obligatory 2.5 children can effect substantial term insurance, permanent health insurance and cover private hospitalisation and specialist medical expenses for less than £500 a year in total.

Five hundred pounds a year is about one twelfth of what statistics tell us most expatriates inject into savings schemes with off-shore unit-linked life assurance companies.

No-one in any of those life companies would, for one second, suggest that it would not be wise for any of their investors to invest a little less in life assurance policies in order to provide for the other insurance needs.

So please speak to your adviser as soon as you can if you do not have all the necessary protection which the insurance and assurance industry can provide.

Best that you are a policy holder rather than just a statistic.

THE UK HOME

HOME SWEET HOME
SUCH IS THE PATRIOT'S BOAST WHERE'ERE HE ROAM HIS FIRST BEST COUNTRY EVER IS AT HOME.

"Home", when you are far away, is an emotive word. Unless great care is displayed in considering all the angles of home-ownership whilst abroad you will find that the emotions the word can engender include anger and disappointment.

A recent survey which I conducted amongst a sizeable sample of working British expatriates revealed that the major financial objective of their going to work abroad was to secure for themselves and their families a worthwhile place to live.

Of those kind enough to take part in the survey over thirty per cent revealed that a bigger house was their objective; nearly forty five per cent had less ambitious intentions. They just wanted to be able to afford a house of their own rather than continue to live with parents or in rented accommodation.

To buy a home or a bigger home or to make radical improvements to an existing home were amongst the top five objectives of all expatriates who took part. To put that in some perspective, other financial goals included paying off outstanding debts, providing enough money to start up a business, paying for the private education of children and securing a better financial base upon which to build a more acceptable life upon return to the UK.

Nearly sixty per cent of all those who already had a home in the UK [albeit bought on mortgage] while working abroad were letting their homes to tenants. Interestingly less than half of that number had their building society's permission to do so; and less than a quarter had done anything to ensure that a UK tax assessment on the rental income was being dealt with.

As I have already explained in the tax chapter **a non-resident working expatriate** should have no fears about the income and capital gains liabilities which he might suffer on his world wide income and assets if he retains accommodation available for his use while he is working abroad. Therefore whether or not to continue to own a home in the UK is not a decision that will be influenced by tax legislation.

Practically every expatriate who already owns a home in the UK will, however, have to decide what action he should take; will he leave it empty, sell it, or let it to tenants whilst he is abroad.

Selling the UK property

A fair number of working expatriates sell their existing UK home before they go abroad to work. Their plan usually involves investing the sale proceeds in some investment media that will grow faster than UK houses are likely to rise and then purchasing a new home once they return. To many expatriates — especially those whose families are living abroad with them — such a move seems a good idea.

Most existing expatriates have found that to sell their home is the worst decision that they could possibly make.

They have overlooked the legal and allied fees involved in a house sale; the problems involved in storing or selling furniture, and the fact that the ever increasing demand for houses tends to mean that over a period of years prices soar. Much of the monetary reward of working overseas for a few years could be wasted if a house sold to-day for £50,000 commands a purchase price of £80,000 or more in five years' time.

I have recently heard of a case in which a man and his family went abroad to

Freemans International of London
139 Clapham Road London SW9 0HR

Initials Surname

Mr/Mrs/Miss ______________________

Address ______________________

____

____

ACT NOW! JUST POST THIS COUPON TODAY. SPECIAL OFFER - ½ PRICE. SEND £3 INSTEAD OF £6.

Freemans International of London
139 Clapham Road London SW9 0HR

Initials Surname

Mr/Mrs/Miss ______________________

Address ______________________

____

____

ACT NOW! JUST POST THIS COUPON TODAY. SPECIAL OFFER - ½ PRICE. SEND £3 INSTEAD OF £6.

Freemans International of London
139 Clapham Road London SW9 0HR

Initials Surname

Mr/Mrs/Miss ______________________

Address ______________________

____

____

ACT NOW! JUST POST THIS COUPON TODAY. SPECIAL OFFER - ½ PRICE. SEND £3 INSTEAD OF £6.

work in 1982 and sold their house in south London for £56,000. They repaid the building society mortgage of £12,000 and invested the balance with a unit trust manager. They returned in 1985 and, for the purposes of work and the children's schooling, decided to look at property in their old neighbourhood. Coincidence being what coincidence very often is, their old house was up for sale; it suited them admirably except in one respect. The asking price was £84,000! They were somewhat hampered in their negotiations by the fact that their investment with the unit trust manager [£40,000 in 1982] was worth £42,000 in 1985. They had liquid cash in an offshore bank account of £20,000 and so repurchased their old home with a new building society mortgage of £22,000; almost twice as much mortgage as they had started with three years previously.

Such a thing happening to you should not be overlooked; nasty things do not always happen to the other fellow.

So, for this reason if no other, the sale of the UK home should be considered very carefully.

Although no "historical" review can accurately predict future trends, all indications show that in general, unless a change of house has already been contemplated, the prospect of working abroad for a time should rarely automatically lead to the selling of the family home.

The alternatives of either leaving the house empty or letting in your absence should be considered; although, as we shall discover, those alternatives are not without their problems either.

Leaving the property in the care of a friend and neighbour seldom proves very satisfactory. Although there are startling examples that show that this arrangement can work; expatriate friends of mine who work in Nigeria have neighbours who not only pop in every evening to turn on lights but cut the grass every week and meet them at the airport when they return home on leave. Such neighbours do not live next door to everyone, more is the pity. Most people have enough problems looking after their own house without taking on the responsibility of an absent friend's.

You can, for a fee, employ an agency to look after the property for you. This can work very well especially if you are likely to make frequent visits back to the UK and might wish to use the house yourself. But this is not a highly satisfactory arrangement for long term expatriates as houses, like other possessions, benefit from care and attention and need to be lived in to keep cold and damp from penetrating and taking hold. Taking hold not only of the fabric of the building but the contents too.

But before you can happily turn to the alternative — that of letting your home — you have to make a judgement based on your own philosophy.

You will have to consider whether you will feel happy about people — total strangers in all probability — using your loo, making love in your bed, laughing about the colour of the sitting room wall paper or cringing about the way you have arranged the kitchen cupboards. Will you mind their children sleeping in your child's bed? Will you feel annoyed when you cannot use the house when you are on leave? That is all for you to decide.

If you decide that you can suffer the possible feeling of "homelessness" then letting the property to tenants might well be a better alternative to leaving the place empty.

Unless the tenants are totally untrained then it is surely a better alternative to selling your home, working abroad for three years and then finding that you have to take out a triple size mortgage to buy it back again.

In what way might tenants be untrained? you might ask.

A couple in Epsom, Surrey, let their home to a "dear old lady who wanted to have somewhere to live for three years before joining her son in Canada; she was so sweet". I quote from a letter I received from this embittered Netherlands-based couple.

The old lady was pretty frail as well: too frail to venture out into the garden on a winter's night to collect coal for the central heating boiler. So, one day in the winter of 1984, she employed two strong lads to move the bunker and the fifteen hundred-weight of coal it contained a little nearer to the boiler; which was in the kitchen. When the expatriates returned to take over their house what did they find? "To our horror we found the coal bunker and its contents in the middle of the kitchen floor; the wooden floor supports have collapsed and we have had to spend £1,200 having the floor replaced". How did they find the tenant in the first place? "We knew her daughter-in-law very well and didn't bother with the cost of an agent".

Another couple, long term expatriates in Bolivia, leased their home to a Bolivian gentleman who was going to work in London for a couple of years. After two years he moved on to Australia leaving a long list of debts and "he had taken down a wall which divided the sitting room from the dining room; the result is that the upstairs floors were on their way down to meet the downstairs". And how did they find their tenant? They met him in a bar in La Paz.

If you take those two examples as being cautionary tales then your first step, if you decide to lease your home in your absence, is to discuss the situation with a competent estate agent. Competent, that is, not only in selling houses but all the ramifications of letting homes in the absence of their owners.

Letting your UK home

It would be foolhardy in the extreme to claim that letting is always a worthwhile proposition. I have tried to point out that there are philosophical as well as financial aspects to be considered. Each individual must decide for himself whether he thinks the possible hassles are worthwhile or not.

Before I counsel you always to employ a proper agent if you decide to rent your home, may I add just one more thing? In my view it is damaging to the psychological well-being of some children based at school in the UK whilst their parents work abroad, to discover that while their parents are two thousand miles away they, the children, have no home available to them in Britain. Not a home that they will of necessity want to use but rather one which they think about when ever they get homesick. A psychologist friend of mine suggests that it is "supportive to a child who is missing his or her parents to know that 'home' remains intact. We all need a hole to run and hide in when the going gets tough, even if we only run to it in our imagination. If the hole is occupied by a strange animal it tends to increase the panic".

I pass on that piece of advice without further comment other than it sounds good common sense to me.

If you decide to let your home to tenants and it is mortgaged to a building society, bank or life assurance company then you must obtain permission to lease the property; permission is normally quite readily given but without it you will undoubtedly be in contravention of your mortgage deed. Write to the society, bank or life company involved; make sure that you quote their roll number or mortgage reference and explain in brief detail why you need to let the house. Indicate the length of time you intend to be working overseas.

Once the necessary permission is granted [sometimes it is granted for a period of the three years at the outset, with your having to re-apply at the end of three years] it is in your best interests to consult an estate agent practising close to your home and discuss with him the terms under which he manages the letting of property for absentee landlords.

The size of his fees will probably be the thing that interests you most; but it should not be. You should be exceedingly interested in the services he is going to provide; the cost of his providing them should be of secondary importance. Many an expatriate has been appalled by the lack of attention which some estate agents pay to the fine details required in the planning of a successful leasing of their home.

The first thing you need to discuss is whether in his opinion there is a ready "market" of potential tenants. I have to assume that you would prefer a tenant who would treat your home with respect. You may wish to dictate that you will only let the property for a specific time; that you will only let it to married couples and, even, that they should have no children under the age of five.

The moment you put constraints on the agent you will cut down the potential number of tenants.

You might be glad to find any tenants at all; if you live on the outskirts of a small town rather than in the centre of a busy city with commercial firms around who require staff to live close by. If you live in a bijou cottage miles from anywhere, with no phone and no bus routes as opposed to a flat convenient to shops and the station, you will find greater difficulty in dictating whom you will allow into the home while you are away.

If you live in a commercially depressed area as opposed to a town within easy reach of London you might not be able to suggest to the agent [more often, he will not be able to suggest it to you] that the ideal tenant will be someone on secondment from abroad, with the firm paying the rent on his behalf.

All these points and many others are matters which must be discussed with the agent before you can actually take any decision.

If, as can quite often happen, the agent has several potential tenants already "on his books" you are little short of half way there to getting him to act for you.

You should enquire of him what "vetting" he has done or will do to obviate any difficulties which can arise by chosing the wrong tenant.

He will undoubtedly require references from them; he will do his best to ensure that they are not likely to misuse your furnishings or run up enormous bills and leave you responsible for them. He will discuss with you the amount of deposit that will be required against the rent or other expenses. He will, or should, ensure that your interests in wishing to return to the property are covered by the protection of the Rent Act.

If he discusses those matters with you, then you are more than half way. But you are not there yet!

He should discuss with you such nitty-gritty detail of inventories, a schedule of dilapidations, insurance, tenancy agreements and, and, and, AND the legal requirement he has to make a return of the rental income for assessment for UK income tax!

If all those points are thoroughly discussed with you then the agent knows what he is doing and will undoubtedly be competent for you to entrust him with your home. It is then that you can make decisions.

What rent are you going to charge?

Many expatriates are guided by their agents on this matter; and, in truth, there is no standard format to determine what a suitable rent is. One intending expatriate wrote to me recently for comment on the fact that an agent he had approached had suggested that a rent of £250 a month [gross] was a reasonable rent for a two bedroomed, semi detached house on the outskirts of Bristol.

My correspondent advised me that he had had this figure from several agents over a period of a few months but that, since he had mortgaged the property up to the hilt, his repayments were in excess of £400 a month and he felt that was a fair rent! What he was asking a tenant to do was to live in the property for a few years and pay considerably over the market price for the privilege.

Obviously the financial aspects of letting must be high on the list of priorities but you have to be sensible.

Rent apart you must take due regard to the other expenses; the rates and water rates; the cost of any major repair work such as decorating or re-wiring. You will have a good idea of what needs doing; you will already have plans for repointing the chimney or replacing fences or that window that always rattles whenever the wind blows.

Consider one point very carefully. You are moving away from and out of your home for a year or two. Others are moving in. It will, however temporarily, become their "home" and your "house". You may have been prepared to live with the odd dilapidation; they may not be so willing; especially at a very high rent.

In practically every page of this book I caution you about using the professional skills that are available to you from specialists. I caution you again here. Use a competent agency; there are lots of them around. They are trained and experienced in the matter; the likelihood is that you are not. Neither is your Mother, your Father or your next door neighbour. Do not appoint them as your letting agent.

Apart from finding you suitable tenants and looking after the property while you are away, any agent is legally obliged to make a return of the rental income to the Inland Revenue and to account to the Inland Revenue for the payment of the tax upon the profits from letting; legally obliged! Legally obliged on pain of penalties if he does not do it!

Appoint a competent agent and ensure that both you and he understand that he has these obligations otherwise, as I shall explain when we reach the taxation aspects, you will have a great deal more to worry about than windows rattling.

You can find a professional agent on recommendation or obtain the name of a local member from The National Association of Residential Letting Agents. With him choose a tenant.

A "home-base" tenant is not always an advantage.

Up and down the length of Britain there are hundreds if not thousands of foreign expatriates assigned to Britain for a while or temporarily re-assigned British expatriates looking for a temporary home. They are in the same boat as you are; somewhere they have a home let to tenants and, with any luck, will treat your house as they hope theirs is being treated. That is a big advantage; the disadvantage may be that they usually have a higher standard in their requirements; the days of letting "tat" for a fortune in rent have gone. Dilapidations in furniture, fittings, fixtures and the fabric of your house will inevitably need to be put right before this sort of tenant is happy to sign on the dotted lines of the tenancy agreement.

The agreement itself will, to some extent, be a flexible arrangement covering the essentials [such as protection for you and your family regarding re-possession of the property] and the individual requirements of you and those to whom you are leasing. I have included a tenancy agreement as an appendix to this chapter. I have done so in the hope that you will skim through it, see the complexities and then take professional advice. I have not done so in any way to encourage you into a do it yourself exercise by inviting your parents or a friend to control the letting for you.

Do not even dream of it; if you do, the dream, I can assure you, will become a nightmare.

Let us break off for a few moments and play a little game together; just to get away from the heaviness of parts of this chapter. If you are already an expatriate who has leased his house in the UK you get ten points for each item you can name; if you are an intending expatriate sitting at home reading this book you get five points.

What you have to do is tell me how many knives, forks and spoons you have in the kitchen drawer, what colour your colander is and how big the crack is just below the tap in the bathroom wash-basin *chez vous*.

Anyone who gets more than one hundred and fifty points is the world champion!

So, before you lease out your house, you should have an inventory made; otherwise how are you going to determine what items you are leaving in the tenant's charge or what condition carpets, curtains and other things are in when left behind?

In its simplest form an inventory is merely a detailed list of the contents of the property. In its fullest form it is also a schedule of the condition of the contents. Untrained people find an inventory very difficult to take; some agents have an "in house" inventory clerk, others will recommend one to you. The fee for the inventory will be about £60 for a small flat and £200 for a family home. A worthwhile expenditure since it will form the basis of any claim against insurers or the tenant.

Insurance

If you require the continued strength of the insurance industry around your house while you are away you must consult your broker or other insurance adviser and inform him that you are leasing the home to tenants while you are away.

All contents belonging to you should be comprehensively covered and you should consider covering specific items under the "all risks" section of the household property.

Certain insurers insist that cover ceases to be in force in the case of "theft not involving forcible entry or violent entry or exit from the premises". This means that if you let your home to me, and I "accidentally" pack one of your valuables when I leave and "forget" to return it, you will not be covered.

Seek proper advice; if you are already an expatriate and have not covered these points then it will be in your interests to do so now.

UK taxation and the UK home

Utopia is a country where there are no strikes, no diseases, people live to a very ripe old age, food is free, booze is free and no cigarette ever does anyone any harm. The sun shines all day and the right amount of rain falls only between midnight and dawn; there is a profusion of flowers and trees, all the kids are very well behaved and no-one ever wants to leave. So they never have to let their homes to tenants and pay the tax consequences.

Then there is the United Kingdom.

In the UK any profit which is made as a result of letting a property is subject

to UK income tax; no matter where in the world the landlord lives and whether or not he is not resident and not ordinarily resident there.

The UK Inland Revenue do not like chasing working British expatriates around the world in the faint hope that they will be given a proper return on the assessable income from the letting so they assess someone in the UK. **If there is an agent involved in the letting he, the agent, is assessed for the tax; if there is not an agent then the liability for the rent falls on the tenant. That is the inescapable law of the United Kingdom.**

The agent does not have to be a professional agent; if you let your home to me and a friend or relative is responsible for the property while you are away then he or she is the agent and receives and must respond to making returns. He or she is assessable for the tax and will be sent the demands for it.

If you do not have any agent, if you have simply leased the house to me and left me responsible for paying the rent into the bank for you or sending you a cheque once a month, then do not expect the full rent from me. I must deduct 29% income tax from the gross rent and pay it to the Revenue when they demand it from me. I am assessable for tax and I will be sent the demands for it.

There is no exception to these rules. The agent is only allowed to forego his responsibilities if you are able to assure the Revenue that some other competent person will accept them.

Tenant's tax responsibilities

I will assume that no-one would be so foolish as to lease his home to me without using a proper agent; and, having found the fool, I will be honest enough not to skip off to the Bahamas with the tax retention and a blonde.

I pay you £300 per calendar month rent; I send you every month £213, keeping £87 a month in the jar beside the kettle in the kitchen.

Every year I make my personal tax return to the Inland Revenue: I tell them how little I have earned from writing books and how much I have had to spend on necessary foreign travel and expensive pencils and word-processors. On the tax return I am asked how much rent I am paying to an absent land-lord. I tell them the truth about that and as swift as an arrow comes back the demand for the tax retention; so I empty out the jar and pay them the cash and that is about the end of it until next year.

I could, of course, tell the Revenue that you have a big mortgage, that you paid for the replacement of the whole of the back porch when it fell down, that you pay the rates, have the garden dug up twice a week, and that you insure the property. But why should I care? I am too busy wondering why they will not believe me that I earn so little and spend so much in necessary expenses.

In all the years that I have been involved with advising expatriates I have not found a situation in which leaving it to the tenant to deal with the tax assessments has proved satisfactory; I can, however, remember several instances where it has proved a headache.

If you insist on leaving out that ingredient which I think is essential, the competent agent, then you should ensure that an accountant or some other fiscal adviser [such as the tax department of your bank] is declared to the Revenue as your rent collecting agency. In that instance the assessment will by-pass the tenant and go directly to someone who can pay — or more probably, dispute — the assessment.

UK tax and the agent

Any agent who manages leased property on behalf of an absent landlord is the person to whom the Inland Revenue turns when an assessment on the rents is calculated.

Often the tax office dealing with the assessment upon the rental income is different from the tax office who previously dealt with the landlord's tax affairs under the PAYE system. If your previous employer was based in London and his PAYE office were a "London Provincial" office as far away as Edinburgh you may find, if your house is in Sussex, that Brighton is the tax office who issues the assessment.

That will mean that although Brighton might know that the property is let and might even know what the rental income is [they can have a good guess if they do not!], they most certainly will be unaware that you have a building society mortgage in Halifax, Skipton, Woolwich or Bristol-and-all-points-West.

They will also not know, unless someone they believe tells them, that you have had a considerable amount of expenditure in necessary repairs, that you pay the rates, what the agent's fees are, how much it costs to insure the property, what necessarily-incurred accountant's fees might be, or indeed the cost of any other allowable deduction is.

It is the assessable profit from the rental income that the Revenue will seek to charge to tax; not the gross rental income. So it inevitably pays to inform your agent [upon whom the charge to tax will be levied] of any of these facts about which he might be unaware.

Armed with the facts the agent can dispute the original assessment, demand a "stay of execution" and prepared accounts with authenticated invoices for expenditure and the amount of the mortgage interest paid.

If you have a mortgage allow the agent to know what the roll number of the building society is; or the reference used by the bank or life assurance company. He can tell the Revenue; they can ask the building society, bank or life company the amount of the interest and re-issue an assessment based on the profits from the rental income net of all these deductions.

There are professional agents, usually smaller estate agents, who categorically refuse to have anything to do with returns to the Inland Revenue by insisting that the landlord appoints someone else to accept the assessment. These agents seem to be perfectly happy to collect anywhere between 10%-17.5% of the rental income for doing very little. Surprisingly working expatriates, particularly those who pride themselves on being "canny", allow this to happen and pay yet more fees to an accountant to do the job that any managing agent should do as a matter of course and as part of his fees.

If the agent is a real managing agent and accepts his responsibilities as he should then he will want to retain a portion of the rents as a safeguard-fund against the liabilities which he knows will arise. Expatriates can sometimes take grave exception to this natural desire of the good managing agent to be in funds for the payment of tax; a funny lot are some expatriates. They shout at the firm doing its job and retain one who is not.

The agent will then only release the excess of the retention once he knows what, if any, allowable deductions can be made.

As I pointed out in the tax chapter MIRAS can be allowed on mortgages upon property which is let to tenants; if yours is such a mortgage then you cannot expect to receive an allowance for mortgage interest again when an assessment is issued against rental income.

Most recent working British expatriates who received MIRAS prior to going abroad to work will find it to their advantage to retain this situation rather than dispense with MIRAS and claim the mortgage interest against the assessment on rental income. If the expatriate is abroad for more than four years MIRAS will inevitably stop; then a claim can be submitted against the rental income when the assessment is raised.

Income tax on rental profits

As I explained in the tax chapter rental income is liable to UK tax wherever in the world the landlord is situated. I also tried to make it clear that not only do the Inland Revenue make every attempt to impose tax on the rent [or rather the assessable profits from the letting] but, through ignorance or sheer silliness, many expatriates do not make return of the income and allowable expenses. Without any doubt at all that is unwise since, invariably, upon their return to the UK those expatriates are discovered, taxed and often penalised.

Remember these important points.

Where rent is payable to a landlord who is not resident for UK tax purposes the Revenue require to assess someone who is in the UK for income tax on the profits from the letting.

The law requires that

1] Where there is an agent of any kind between the tenant and the landlord [or the landlord's bank account!] the agent must assume ultimate responsibility for a] the preparation of the accounts on which any liability to tax will be assessed and b] for paying that tax when the demand is issued.

2] Where the tenant pays the rent direct to the landlord [or to his bank account] then the tenant is assessable for income tax at the base rate. He must deduct 29% from the rent and account for it to the Collector of Taxes each year. Not he should, but he MUST; otherwise he will be penalised.

If, as I say, the landlord has an agent of any kind [perhaps a member of his family living close by to the property] then it is vital to ensure that the agent is aware of the Revenue's requirements and is prepared to receive special income tax return forms for completion each year.

Where no agent exists and the rent is paid direct to the landlord by the tenant then that tenant is legally responsible for deducting the tax. Even if the tenant does not know that he has these responsibilities the Revenue will still look to him for payment. The tenant in these circumstances may have already paid the rent gross and will not have anything in reserve. It is not at all unusual in such circumstances for the tenant, having woken up, to with-hold future rent until the assessment is made good.

I stress the fact that no non-resident landlord escapes a liability to UK tax on the profit from the letting of property in the UK. No-one, whatever his or her nationality or domicile.

So it is very worthwhile making sure that an agent is employed to make these returns. I have told you that some agents tell their landlord clients that they do not provide such a service; the landlord client [you perhaps?] should point out that under the Taxes Act the agent has the legal responsibility to make the returns.

He should point it out as he slams the door of the estate agent's office and goes to find another one! Too many agents get wealthy without working for their money in this regard; far too many. And far too many expatriates allow them to.

The assessable profit from the rents will be calculated by deducting from the gross rents received the following allowable expenditures.

a] general and water rates when paid by the landlord
b] other services [electricity, gas, gardener, TV rental, window cleaners, etc.] maintained at the landlord's expense for the benefit and use of the tenant
c] buildings insurance premiums
d] necessary repairs to the fabric of the buildings or the fittings
e] redecoration
f] ground rents or other annual charges
g] agent's commission and fees [including VAT]
h] agent's extraneous disbursements such as the preparation of letting agreements and inventories.

Where the letting is a furnished letting the following may be added:

j] contents insurance premiums
k] repairs to, regular servicing of or replacement of [but not repairs to] hard furnishing

l] a "non-expense"; depreciation of soft furnishings, fixed at 10% of the gross rents receivable minus the sums claimed under a] and b] above.

Additionally, and usually most importantly, interest paid on a qualifying mortgage on the property can be offset against the gross rents.

I have already pointed out that if you are claiming MIRAS you cannot get the relief for interest twice; you will have already enjoyed it as you paid the mortgage.

Some expatriates consider that the best investment they can make is to plough all their spare capital into the purchase of UK residential property and then to let it out to tenants. Often they take out loans to complete the purchase price.

Unless such purchases are made under the direction of a reputable agent, in an area where both high rental income and acceptable capital growth is practically assured, then such investments can prove dreadful.

Rarely do any but the most fastidious of agents, jealous of their reputation, point out the high costs of legal and allied fees involved in the purchase of the property [as well as its eventual sale], the possibilities of substantial costs in maintaining and insuring the property or the tax consequences. Tax consequences which involve not only income tax but potential CGT liabilities.

Capital gains tax on UK property

Property, like any other asset sold at a profit, can be assessed for CGT upon its sale unless the owner is not resident and not ordinarily resident in the UK at the time of its sale and is not disposing of the property during a year for part of which he was regarded as ordinarily resident [unless he has been not resident and not ordinarily resident for at least 36 months].

I suggest you refer back to the tax chapter if that summary does not remind you of the salient points of CGT exemptions.

Therefore, if you wish to invest in UK property in the hope that it is going to rise in value and you are going to be abroad for less than 36 months, it has to rise pretty high and pretty fast for you to make the money you have promised yourself free of CGT.

Letting your UK home can force upon you a CGT liability on its eventual sale too unless at the time of the sale you are not resident and not ordinarily resident as I have just described OR the property was only let for a period [not exceeding four years] that you were prevented from occupying the house because you were working in a foreign location.

There are many individual circumstances which can dictate whether or not the letting of UK property will give rise to an eventual CGT liability. I have tried to convince you several times that individual circumstances affect the way in which tax law is applied; they do not affect the law which is the same for everybody.

I can but emphasise, yet again, the need for you to get professional advice and to take that advice long before you make any decision which can affect your UK tax liabilities. Decisions made in haste are usually made in error; give your adviser, be he accountant, solicitor or tax counsellor at your bank or stockbroker, time to give you the full facts upon which a rational decision can be made.

Please do not, as I discovered a little while ago that a group of thirty expatriates all working in one location did, write to the Inland Revenue direct and ask their opinion concerning your potential tax liability. The Revenue will undoubtedly tell you; they know all the answers. But as I have said before, a competent tax adviser knows the answers too and may suggest ways of mitigating the problems that could arise.

Were we face to face I would force you to remember the art of caution by telling you an old Russian folk tale about a blackbird, a cow and a cat. But I cannot do so in a book; if you do not know the story and wish to know it, write to me. You have my address.

Just as the Revenue now have the address of the thirty expatriates.

As I promised in the body of this chapter I have added this appendix as a guide to the Rent Act which, apart from anything else, governs the letting of property by expatriates whilst they are working abroad.

Part of the rules which the Rent Act encompasses impose restrictions on the landlord re-possessing the property. Basically he can only do so at the end of the letting:

a] where he has owned and occupied the property as his home prior to the commencement of the letting and has given an appropriate notice to the tenant prior to the tenant's occupation on commencement of the tenancy that he will require the house for his own [or his family's] residence.

b] where he acquired the house with a view to occupying it as his home on retirement and has given the appropriate notice to the tenant prior to the tenant's occupation and now wants to live there.

c] where a "short hold" lease was created within the terms of the Housing Act 1980.

I have used more formal language to explain the problems in order to underline the essential need for you to consult a lawyer on all matters of leasing your home to tenants while you are away. It will not cost a fortune for you to do so and may well save you one in legal fees when you try vainly to remove a tenant who insists on sitting there once you have returned.

Points a] and b] above are now modified somewhat by your being able to re-possess the house if it is no longer suitable for your needs and you wish to sell with vacant possession and buy another property for use as your own residence. Modified or not the rules are complex and you really should ensure that the tenancy agreement is given the blessing of your solicitor before it is signed by either party **and** that no possession of the premises should be given to any tenant before the agreement has been legally vetted and signed.

As promised I have included in this appendix a specimen agreement; I repeat that I have done so simply to point out the complexities involved and in no way to encourage you to attempt any short cuts.

Appendix

Specimen agreement for the letting of furnished property

MEMORANDUM OF AGREEMENT made this day of One thousand nine hundred and BETWEEN of (hereinafter called 'the Landlord' which expression where the context admits includes the persons for the time being entitled in reversion expectant on the tenancy hereby created) of the one part and of (hereinafter called 'the Tenant' which expression where the context admits includes the persons deriving title under the Tenant) of the other part

WHEREBY the Landlord agrees TO GRANT a tenancy of and the Tenant agrees TO ACCEPT a letting of all that messuage and dwellinghouse belonging thereto and known as

in the County of (hereinafter called 'the premises') together with the use therein of the fixtures furniture and other contents belonging to the Landlord and specified in an Inventory to be signed by the parties hereto or their accredited Agents upon the following terms and conditions.

(1) THE TENANCY is to be for a period of from the day of One thousand nine hundred and to the day of One thousand nine hundred and

(2) THE RENT to be paid shall be the sum of the first of such payments to be made on the signing of this Agreement and before possession is given provided that if and whenever the amount of general and water rates payable in respect of the said premises shall be increased from the amount payable as at the date hereof then such annual rent shall be increased with effect from the 1st April when such changes take place by the amount of such increase.

(3) THE TENANT agrees with the Landlord as follows:

(a) TO PAY the said rent at the times and in the manner aforesaid without any abatement or deduction whatsoever.

(b) TO TAKE due and proper care of the furniture and effects and to keep the same and the said premises in the same state and condition as they are in on entry and so surrender the same at the expiration or sooner determination of the tenancy fair wear and tear and damage by accidental fire excepted.

(c) TO REPLACE such articles as may be broken lost chipped stained cracked or otherwise injured or damaged during the tenancy or alternatively to pay the fair value thereof.

(d) TO PAY for the cleaning and washing of such articles as may require washing or cleaning at the expiration or sooner determination of the tenancy due regard being paid to their condition on entry and to sweep the chimneys and clean the windows as often as necessary and TO LEAVE the windows clean and the chimneys swept.

(e) TO KEEP and leave the water and waste pipes attached to the cistern water closets and sinks and also drains gutters and rainwater pipes free and clear from all obstructions and in as good working order as they are in on his taking possession latent defects and fair wear and tear excepted and take all necessary precautions against damage by frost keeping the premises properly heated during cold weather and to make good all damage occasioned due to his neglect or omission to keep the premises properly heated.

(f) TO PAY the cost of the telephone rent and for all calls and services made during the tenancy and to pay for all electricity gas or other fuel used or consumed during the tenancy including any standing charge for electricity or gas and meter rents.

(g) NOT TO ASSIGN underlet or part with possession of the premises or any part thereof and not to leave the premises unoccupied for any period in excess of   weeks during the tenancy.

(h) NOT TO REMOVE any of the said furniture and effects or any part thereof respectively from the premises under any pretext whatsoever and to leave the furniture and effects at the expiration of the tenancy arranged in such order as at the commencement of the tenancy.

(i) TO USE the premises for the purpose of a private dwelling-house only and not to do or permit to be done any act matter or thing which may make void or voidable any Policy or Policies of Insurance which the Landlord may have effected upon the premises or contents thereof or render any extra premium payable in respect thereof.

(j) NOT TO do or permit to be done any act matter or thing that will be or become a nuisance or annoyance or damage to the Landlord or the owners or occupiers of the adjoining premises.

(k) TO GIVE notice to the Landlord or his or Agents of any infectious disease happening or breaking out in the said premises during the tenancy and to pay the cost of disinfection or any other subsequent expense caused to the Landlord by such illness.

(l) NOT TO cut lop or injure or remove any timber or timberlike trees or shrubs that may be growing or standing on the premises and to stock keep cultivate maintain and tend the garden and mow the lawns and use the garden in a proper manner and so to keep and leave the same at the expiration or sooner determination of the tenancy in the same state and conditions as on entry according to the season of the year and subject to the remarks in the Inventory.

(m) NOT TO keep any domestic animals upon the premises without the previous written consent of the Landlord.

(n) TO ALLOW the Landlord or his or her Agents to view the premises at reasonable hours of the day once during every month upon forty-eight hours notice being given and to permit access for workmen to carry out any repairs that are needful to preserve the property.

(o) TO PERMIT prospective Tenants or Purchasers to view the premises during the last three months of the tenancy at all reasonable hours of the daytime by previous appointment.

(p) TO PAY on the signing of this Agreement and before possession the sum of   to the Landlord's Agents as security or deposit for any dilapidations or any charges that may accrue and for which the Tenant is liable and the said sum shall be held by the Agents until the end of the tenancy and shall then be applied towards the payment of dilapidations or charges as aforesaid and any balance not so used shall be refunded to the Tenant.

(4) THE LANDLORD AGREES AS FOLLOWS:

a] TO PAY all rates and taxes and other assessments except the charges for electricity gas telephone and fuel which are or which may be payable during the tenancy.

b] TO KEEP the exterior of the premises wind and watertight during the tenancy.

c] TO INSURE and keep insured the premises and contents against loss or damage by fire.

(d) THE TENANT duly paying the said rent and performing all the stipulations and conditions hereinbefore contained shall have and enjoy peaceable possession of the premises during the period aforesaid without interruption by the Landlord or any person lawfully claiming under him or her.

(5) IT IS MUTUALLY AGREED between the parties hereto:

(a) THAT in the event of the rent or any part thereof being unpaid for a period of Fourteen days after the same shall have become due and payable whether legally demanded or not or in the event of a breach by the Tenant of any of the conditions and stipulations herein contained it shall be lawful for the Landlord or his or her Agents to re-enter and re-take possession of the premises without prejudice to his or her rights to all rent then in arrear or any damages for breach of this Agreement.

(b) IF THE premises or any part shall at any time during the tenancy be destroyed by fire so as to be unfit for habitation and use and the Policy or Policies of Insurance effected by the Landlord shall not have been vitiated or payment of the Policy monies refused in whole or in part in consequence of any act of default of the Tenant the rent hereby reserved or a fair proportion thereof according to the nature and extent of the damage sustained shall be suspended until the premises shall again be rendered fit for habitation and use and any dispute concerning this Clause shall be determined by a single Arbitrator in accordance with the Arbitration Act 1950 or any statutory enactments in that behalf for the time being in force.

(c) The Landlord hereby notifies the Tenant that the Landlord is the owner-occupier [owner] of the premises within the meaning of Case 11 [12] Schedule 15 of The Rent Act 1977 and that the premises may be recovered by the Landlord under the said Case 11 [12] as amended and by virtue of Section 98 of the Rent Act 1977. AS WITNESS the hands of the said parties the day and year first hereinbefore written.

Witness to the Signature of the Said
....
Witness ....
Address ....
....
....
Occupation..

To emphasise in the tenant's mind the eventual need of the expatriate for the vacant possession of his house, it is legally advisable that a letter along the following lines is also sent to the tenant and acknowledged by him.

Specimen letter to the tenant from the landlord

Dear (tenant)
Re: (Address of Property)
I hereby give you Notice that I am an owner-occupier [owner] within the meaning of the Rent Act 1977.
I shall require possession for my own occupation at the expiration of the tenancy which I am about to grant to you and I am entitled to recover such possession by reason of Case 11 [12] of the Fifteenth Schedule to the Rent Act 1977.
Yours faithfully,
Dated
I hereby acknowledge receipt of a copy of the above Notice

....
(Signature of tenant)

CHILDREN'S EDUCATION

Special attention has to been given to the educational problems of the children of working expatriates.

It is not always possible or indeed advisable for anyone going to work abroad to take children of school age with him because

a] **there may be no English speaking schools available**

b] **the foreign country may have an education system totally dissimilar from that of the UK**

c] **local education in the foreign country may be very expensive**

d] **the children may be at a crucial point in their UK education; just beginning secondary school or about to take O and A level examinations.**

Many expatriates who go abroad to work on secondment from their UK employers find that included in their emoluments package is either the offer to pay the entire private school fees or the provision of substantial financial support. Employers recognise the fact that in many countries of the world the local education is so different from that to which the child has been used to that their paying part or all of the fees to allow the child to remain in Britain in private education is part of their duty to the whole family.

If this is the situation in which you find yourself you will have to consider very carefully

a] **whether your child will happily bear separation from you and, just as important, whether you will be able to settle in your new surroundings parted from him or her;**

b] **whether the support you receive is going to stop once you are back in the UK. Is the child to continue at fee paying school at your expense [if the employer provides support when you are in the UK it becomes a taxable emolument]? Are you going to make your first priority from your saving the funding of fees from the date your employer's grant ceases** and

c] **what will happen if the child becomes ill and needs contact with and comfort from you, its parents.**

The decision can only be made by the family unit.

Children, as every parent knows, are peculiar creatures. Many would delight in the excitement and adventure of going abroad, learning a new language and meeting new friends. Several expatriate families I know have been delighted with the results of educating their children at Dutch speaking state schools in Holland. Apart from an initial hiccup when the child was struggling with a syllabus in a language which made demands upon both his intelligence and abilities to wrap his tongue round nigh on unpronounceable words, none of the children of these families has suffered a set-back in their learning curve. But then all of the children were between five and seven years old; the story might well have been quite different had they been in their early teens and intent on the final stages of their schooling.

In such cases where there are no international schools in which lessons are taught in English there might be little alternative other than the child remaining at school in England.

Leaving children in the UK

Should your emoluments package not contain school fee support then you have to consider very hard indeed the situation with your children. Can you afford to put them into fee-charging schools? Will you be able to support them there once you have returned to the UK to find yourself not earning as much? Can they remain in their present school and be looked after by relatives or friends?

The Education Act 1944 does give local authorities the powers to assist parents in the payment of boarding school fees; the powers even extend to the payment of grants to relatives or friends towards the up-keep of children who will go on attending state schools while their parents are abroad. Unfortunately having the power does not necessarily mean having the wherewithal to exercise them; recent UK Government policy has been to cut back to the marrow of the bone the monies available to local authorities for education.

But talking to the Education Officer of the local authority costs little; talk to him and see what, if anything, is available.

If funds are available from any source and the decision is made to leave children back home in fee paying schools then you will need to obtain expert advice on the type of school most suitable for your child.

Expert counselling is available; the best known source of help is that supplied by Gabbitas-Thring. This long established authority on the subject will also help with finding a suitable "guardian" family to look after the child on half-term holidays or weekend exeats.

Taking children abroad

In some English speaking countries [South Africa and the United States, for example] local education is free but in many non-English speaking countries it can be very expensive.

Considering that Britain has for many decades provided a high proportion of the world's expatriate population successive British Governments have done little — indeed you might think, nothing — to emulate the pattern of schools subsidised by the American and French Governments in most parts of the world.

The experience of many expatriates is that the foreign based English speaking schools around the world [with certain remarkable exceptions] do not maintain a particularly high standard but, perforce, charge very high fees.

Some working expatriates have found that until the child reaches secondary school age he or she may "get by" being educated abroad but that once examinations loom on the horizon the decision to allow the child to remain abroad become acute. He either has to return to a fee charging school in the UK or one of the parents [mother normally gets the job] has to return from abroad while the child is attending state school.

Again, people like Gabbitas-Thring can assist; they know what sort of schools are available in the country to which you are going, the sort of fees charged and the examinations which are set. They will know a great deal more than you do, so, if education of your children is causing a headache, consult them.

Deep philosophical and psychological problems can result from leaving a child who had before attended day school back in Britain at boarding school. His surroundings will be as unfamiliar to him as your new surroundings will be to you; even though you might have been briefed as to what to expect. There are practical problems too; the greatest, as I say, is whether upon your return to the UK you will have sufficient money to go on paying for the child's education at a fee charging school.

Around the world there are thousands of working British expatriates who are on a school fees tread-mill; having started their children off in boarding school whilst they are working abroad they are loth to return to the UK and disturb the children's learning pattern. So they keep working abroad; maybe for many years

longer than they ever intended or wanted to. The problems of removing a child from boarding school and returning it to the local comprehensive monolith with forty or more children of mixed abilities to a class have to be experienced to be believed.

I am not the product of the public school system; I was lucky to be in my teens when the local Grammar school was in being. So I have no axe to grind. Grammar schools, like village greens, road verges scattered with marguerites, and proper tin dustbins are things of the past; now replaced by comprehensive schools, dent resisting crash barriers and black plastic bags.

If while you are working abroad your children attend fee charging schools then you must, for their sake, either save sufficient cash or make assurance provision for their further education when you return to the UK or, as many of your fellow expatriates do, get used to being on the tread-mill.

Funding for future school fees

There are, fundamentally, only three ways of paying school fees once you have returned to the UK.

The first is to ensure that you return to a job the emoluments of which are going to be high enough for you to afford the fees as part of your normal family expenditure; if you can guarantee that happy event then you may feel that you have little use for any one of the other two methods; **if you can guarantee that happy event!**

The second is to save a sufficiently large capital sum against which you may draw future school fees; remember, will you not, that the interest earned by that sum of money will be subjected to UK tax once you have returned to the UK. Say, for example, that your only child will be fifteen years old when you return to the UK. You know what the fees are now; what shall we say, with extras [oh! those extras!] £1,750 a term? You will be faced with a total bill of £15,750; that is £1,750 x 3 x 3. Cash in the bank of £13,000 earning 7% net of tax when you start to pay the fees will just about see you through; occasional topping-up from your back pocket of course, but the major part of the fees will be available.

Specialist advisers, such as the renowned School Fees Insurance Agency, will be able to provide a better "investment" for such a lump sum of money; indeed they will be able to suggest schemes which will even allow you to keep your child at school by paying a smaller lump sum and borrowing the remainder.

SFIA will also be able to advise you if you are wise enough to think about the future far enough in advance and plan properly for the payment of school fees through assured plans. Spreading the cost in this way might well be a viable alternative to keeping your sore feet pounding on the tread-mill for a further ten years or so.

Even if you are a long term working expatriate with the greatest confidence in being able to fund future school fees from earnings [may be with your employer's support] or from savings you will make from excess income do not, please, overlook the fact that your death or disability will place a heavy burden on your family resources. In the chapter on insurance I have tried to show how reasonable are the premiums for Family Income Benefit and Permanent Health Insurances.

If you are faced with a long line of future school fee bills consider very carefully your need to effect these vital covers to ensure your children's future education.

THE FRIENDLY ISLANDS

SOME
SECRETED ISLAND
HEAVEN KNOWS WHERE.

History has dictated it, usage over centuries has confirmed it and Wordsworth's words describe it. Off the coast of the United Kingdom nestle Islands where the financial wellbeing of expatriates is an essential part of the way of life.

By some strange quirks, buried deep in constitutional history, there exist four major, low tax, financial areas around the coast of Britain. Since none of them charges tax upon the income or capital gains accrued within its shores by a person who is not resident there, these fiscally-advantageous Islands well merit the title "*friendly*" in the eyes of working British expatriates who are not resident for UK tax purposes.

Alphabetically they are Alderney, Guernsey, the Isle of Man and Jersey. I hope that I shall be offending no-one's sensibilities if I suggest that, were I to have arranged the Islands in order of international recognition, the list would have been reversed.

From time to time noises have been made, both in the British Parliament and outside it, that some future Socialist government ought cancel the advantages with which the Channel Islands and the Isle of Man are blessed. Not so much as a move against the Islands but in order to negate assumed "naughtiness" by UK residents who might use the low tax areas for under-hand, nefarious financial activities.

What people who make such silly remarks forget is that none of the Islands would welcome the fact that its banks or other financial institutions were being used for these purposes and would "weedout" the unwelcomed financial fiddles a lot faster and a lot more effectively than any Member of Parliament.

No official of any one of the Islands has given me permission to say what I am about to say; none would even discuss the matter with me but I am convinced that it will take a great deal more than stupidity on the part of some radical politician to alter the course of nigh on two thousand years of history; particularly constitutional history. I could foresee the banning of fish and chip shops in cockney London happening first.

Sometime in the distant future something might happen to make banking, saving or investing through the Channel Islands or the Isle of Man less advantageous to the working British expatriates; who is to say? But I doubt if it will be as a result of any socialist pressure. Until it does I suggest that, if you have any worries that you might be affected by legislative changes of this sort whilst you are working overseas, you concern yourself about something else.

I have contributed the section on Jersey myself but comment on Alderney, Guernsey and the Isle of Man has been made by contributors who live there; I am grateful for their co-operation in explaining the role which each Island can play in the fiscal and financial aspects of your monetary well-being whilst you are working overseas.

As far as I know the other contributors each has two things in common; they live and work in the areas which they are writing about and each has been nagged into writing by me.

As you read through this chapter section by section you will be struck by other similarities. You will find that each writes of the political and economic stability of his Island; of the professional skills and ethics and low tax advantages of banking and investing there. You will also notice that apart from occasional "asides" none of us takes a swipe at his competitor Islands. The Islands do compete, believe you me!

What you might also notice is one nuance and wonder why it occurs. You may wonder why it is that each of us refers to the Island upon which we work and the Islands upon which the others work as Islands with a capital "I". I did not "sub-edit" these capital letters; they appeared, quite naturally, in each script.

For any of us to have done anything other than use the word Island would have been as unloving and as disrespectful as referring to our or each other's Mother as "mother".

ALDERNEY

contributed by Roger Featherstone FCA

Director, York House Ltd.

"Alderney, where's that? Is that the one with no cars? No! That's Sark, isn't it. So where is Alderney? Is it in Jersey? And do you still have those lovely cows?"

The Milne cows left before the war, but Alderney still flourishes; everyone has heard of Jersey and Guernsey and many have heard of Sark and Alderney but are none too sure where either of the latter two is.

Alderney is the most northerly of the Channel Islands and is approximately three miles long by one mile wide, nine miles from the coast of Normandy and sixty miles from the English mainland. The population of two thousand fiercely independent "locals" and "settlers" live in St Anne's; a town of both Norman and South West England architectural influences.

Alderney's two major historical traumas, the British military presence in the 19th and early 20th centuries and the evacuation of the population in anticipation of occupation by the German invading forces during the Second World War, have diluted the Norman-Alderney indigenes and the local "patois" has now almost completely disappeared.

Of all the Channel Islands Alderney is undoubtedly the most scenically beautiful.

The beaches, cliff walks and small wooded valleys are a delight to the holiday visitor who eschews the crowded razzmatazz of her larger cousins.

There is a story that after the war the Island's President, Toby Herivel, attended a conference convened by the British Government to determine Alderney's political future. The then Governor-General of Jersey rather pompously commented that "Alderney is the Cinderella of the Channel Islands" at which Toby retorted "and you'll remember that Cinderella had two ugly sisters!"

Government and Legislation

Alderney comes within the Bailiwick of Guernsey and her Government is provided by the States; twelve elected, unpaid members under the elected President. At the time of writing there are four women among the twelve, surely the highest proportion anywhere in the world, and a promise of sound government. There are no political parties and thus decisions arrived at tend to represent the concensus view of the populace. One aspect of statehood peculiar to us is the Peoples' Meeting at which all proposed legislation is presented to the public in general meeting and questions and opinions on any aspect of it may be raised.

The States provide a range of public services appropriate to the Island's size and position, and their administration is controlled by committees of members of the States with much of the budget expenditure controlled by the equivalent committees of Guernsey's States.

Justice is administered by the Court, comprising seven Jurats appointed by the United Kingdom Home Office, which meets each week and is the equivalent of an English magistrate's court. The more serious cases and appeals are heard in Guernsey's Royal Court.

Alderney's laws are a strange blend of old Norman-French and the newer English law; they combine the quaint with the pragmatic. Crime is rare, with regular Court reports seldom featuring more than minor motoring or tree-felling offences. It is a refreshing feature of life here that few people lock their doors, cars are usually parked with the keys left in the ignition, and the visiting policemen from the Guernsey force are bored with their term of duty and long to return home for more exciting duties.

Taxation

All taxation is administered on Alderney's behalf by Guernsey's Tax Office and thus the taxation system is almost identical to that of Guernsey. Income tax is levied at 20% on both companies and individuals who are resident as well as upon the income of non-residents which arises in the Bailiwick — rents from property they might own here for example.

The exception to that rule — and of vital importance to working expatriates — is

that interest on Alderney bank accounts held by non-residents is not subject to local tax. For resident individuals our income tax is chargeable upon gross income less admissable charges against that income, as well as certain personal allowances and reliefs.

Resident companies are liable to income tax on agreed adjusted profits after deduction of various allowable items. **A company is non-resident in the Bailiwick if it is managed and controlled outside the Bailiwick and is not beneficially owned by a Bailiwick resident. Such non-resident companies are then liable only to Corporation tax at the rate of £300 per annum.**

There are no higher rates of tax on income, no capital gains or capital transfer taxes, no estate duties or inheritance taxes nor value added tax. The Bailiwick of Guernsey has double taxation agreements with both the United Kingdom and Jersey.

Indirect taxes comprise low excise duties on alcohol, tobacco, petrol and motor vehicles as well as minor licencing and registration fees. Local rates are charged on householders, with an average four bedroomed house giving rise to a liability of approximately £120 per annum in general and water rates.

Expatriate Services

What are the attractions of the Channel Islands to you as an expatriate?

You will have noticed in the financial services world there are various "financial centres" [tax havens, to most of us] which offer safe and prosperous investment bases for your hard earned savings. Switzerland, Bermuda, Cayman Islands, Gibraltar and, even more exotic, Andorra, the Dutch Antilles and Panama all seek to attract your investment with promises of riches to come.

But remember, most of you come from and are likely to return to the United Kingdom, and your financial arrangements while abroad should take account of this ultimate return to your homeland. The UK Inland Revenue have laid various traps to catch the unwary homecomer, laden down with his savings which are supposed to provide the down-payment on that rose-covered cottage in the country. The tax planning for your return should take place before your return, not after the arrival of that buff-coloured OHMS envelope from your local Inspector of Taxes.

The Channel Islands' financial industries are usually well versed in the UK's tax laws amd their application to the returning expatriate. Remember the old adage; "If God had meant us to pay tax, He would not have created the Channel Islands".

Remember also that they enjoy almost unrivalled political and economic stability which should be a prime consideration when choosing the repository for your savings. Almost all participants in the financial services industry in the Islands are governed by the ethical rules of their UK-based professional bodies and also by the Channel Island's own internal regulatory laws.

The Islands are easy and pleasant to visit during your leave in the UK to discuss your affairs with your advisers, and probably the most important advantage the Islands possess is that their local language is English!

What, specifically, can Alderney offer the expatriate?

We have a much higher proportion of settlers than the other Islands and the professional advisers are thus more used to dealing with the taxation and other problems of emigrants from the United Kingdom. We have to subscribe to the Schumacher dictum, "Small is beautiful" in both scenery and financial services. All the major UK clearing banks are represented, offering banking facilities for both local and non-resident customers.

There are two resident accountancy practices offering taxation and investment advice as well as normal accountancy services, and an insurance brokerage with many years experience in the expatriate field. A locally based expatriate services company provides a range of financial services which are tailor made to suit each client's needs. The major offshore funds are represented by local agents, and an internationally recognised Alderney-based company advises on the formation and administration of trusts in the Channel Islands and elsewhere.

Legal advice is provided by an Alderney advocate and the specialised knowledge of United Kingdom solicitors can be obtained speedily.

All business here is transacted in a friendly, relaxed way; which sometimes belies to the outsider the quality of the service.

Permanent Residence

I meet many expatriates every year and one recurrent theme comes into conversations with those approaching or even past retirement; the determination not to live back in the United Kingdom. This is not due to a loss of patriotism; often the home country, left behind twenty years or more ago, has ceased to be recognisable; swamped as it is by motorways, shopping precincts, industrialisation, strikes and riots; all of which appear to the homecomer as the less desirable benefits of progress.

Many try Spain or Portugal; but they miss being close to Britain for visiting relatives and friends.

While Jersey [particularly] and Guernsey have introduced measures making it difficult if not impossible for the retiring expatriates to buy a house on either Island, Alderney still offers an interesting selection of properties available to anyone holding a passport issued in the United Kingdom, European Community or other Channel Islands. Currently the prices range from £30,000 for a "retirement" bungalow to £200,000 for the most spacious converted farmhouse in its own grounds.

The house market is served by four resident estate agencies, who will post details of houses on the market to anywhere in the world, collect the intending buyer from the airport and conduct him around available properties. There are houses to suit most tastes: tastefully converted townhouses to bungalows with panoramic views of the sea.

To the retiring, entitled to the UK state pension, settlement in Alderney means continuing entitlement to the annual increments to the pension.

But mere pecuniary consideration aside, Alderney offers a lifestyle more closely akin to that of many expatriate postings. The pace of life is leisurely and informal [suits are only worn by visiting bank managers and insurance salesmen!]; Alderney people are genuinely friendly and neighbourly and the UK is just forty minutes flying time away for those who occasionally feel island-claustrophobia.

The cliffs, bays and beaches offer spectacular scenery to the walker with some species of wild life almost unique in the British Isles. Telecommunications are excellent and Alderney has its own airline, Aurigny Air Services, operating a fleet of friendly yellow Trislanders and Islanders with Alderney's lion rampant on the tailfin. They link Alderney with Southampton, Bournemouth, Cherbourg and the other Channel Islands, from where connections can be made to Paris and other parts of the Continent.

The climate is equable with frost and snow a rarity; one is immediately struck by the clean, clear air and Summer days seem longer, sunnier and hotter than on the mainland. We are served by a surprisingly fine mix of restaurants offering from "cheap and cheerful" to haute cuisine. For the sports enthusiast facilities are available for cricket, soccer, tennis, sailing, golf, bowls, squash, badminton and fishing. The social life of the Island centres around the fourteen pubs, the golf and sailing clubs, and the music, drama and art clubs. The licensing laws, 10.00 a.m. to 1.00 a.m. in the Summer, are the Channel Island's most lenient, and in any of the bars you can expect to meet interesting locals or visitors from Britain and mainland Europe with Braye Bay a charming sight in August when it is full of moored boats.

Alderney maintains its own cottage hospital, two private medical practices and other medical and dental services sufficient for most requirements. In case of emergency or serious medical needs patients are sent by air to the excellent hospital in Guernsey or, in direst cases to the UK. There is a school giving education to the Island's children from the age of five through to sixteen; while those with academic potential attend one of the secondary schools of high reputation in Guernsey.

If you are looking for an alternative to the rush and bustle of twentieth century life where service is a pleasure for both the server and the served, have a look at Alderney and see if you could stand the pace! It was succinctly summed up once in the observation "in Alderney you seldom hear a child cry".

GUERNSEY

Norman Le Cheminant,
Chief Executive, Advisory and Finance Committee.

The Bailiwick

The Bailiwick of Guernsey comprises the adjacent islets of Herm and Jethou, together with Alderney and Sark. In the Bailiwick there is a Lieutenant-Governor, who is the personal representative of the Sovereign and the official channel of communication between the United Kingdom and the insular authorities. In Guernsey the Bailiff, who is appointed by the Crown, presides over the Royal Court and the legislature and is the head of the Island Administration.

Geography

Guernsey is situated off the north-west coast of France in the Gulf of St Malo, approximately 80 miles (143 kilometres) south of Weymouth. Its varied scenery includes the rocky coastline of the high zone of south Guernsey, where steep indented cliffs give way to valleys running down to the bays often covered with fine granite sand, the wide sandy beaches and low headlands of the remaining coastal districts and the undulating farmland of the Island interior.

The climate of the Island is mild. In winter the mean temperature is 6 degrees centigrade (43 degrees fahrenheit) and in summer 17 degrees centigrade (63 degrees fahrenheit). Sunshine averages between 1,800 and 2,000 hours a year and the rainfall under 35 inches (91.5 centimetres) a year.

Area and Population

The most westerly of the main Islands, Guernsey has an area of about 24 square miles (62 square kilometres) and a population of approximately 54,000.

History

The Islands were integrated into the Duchy of Normandy in the tenth and eleventh centuries and became dependencies of the English Crown when their Duke William became King of England in 1066.

When continental Normandy was overrun by the King of France, in 1204, the Islands remained in the hands of the King of England, who continued to govern them in his capacity as Duke of Normandy, until he surrendered the title in 1259.

Thereafter the Sovereign continued to rule the Islands as though he were Duke of Normandy, observing their laws and customs and liberties. These were later confirmed by the charters of successive sovereigns, which secured the Islands their own judiciaries, freedom from process of English courts, free trade with the United Kingdom and certain other privileges.

After the separation of the Islands from Normandy and its administration, the local institutions were gradually moulded, very largely on local initiative, to meet changing circumstances until their present constitutions evolved.

Since 1204 the Islands have been attacked by French forces on a number of occasions during hostilities between France and England. They were occupied by Germany during the Second World War.

Language

English is now the language in daily use, although the French patois is still spoken by some people.

Self-Governing for Stability

If there is one quality above all others which tends to foster and encourage economic growth — it is stability.

Guernsey, through its independence and unusual constitution, enjoys a unique political stability, and this happy state of affairs has been a basic factor in the Island's prosperity and economic growth.

General Political and Economic Profile

Guernsey is a self-governing dependency of the English Crown. Although the United Kingdom is responsible for the foreign relations and external defence of the Island, Guernsey is politically independent and has its own legislature, the States of Deliberation. No political parties are represented in the States, and the administration of Government is carried out through a number of Committees each of which is responsible for a particular service or function such as Health, Education, Finance, etc. The political independence of the elected representatives and the absence of Cabinet government means that general elections are not followed by marked changes in policies, and there is no doubt that Guernsey's current prosperity and economic strength is a result of its long history of political stability.

Guernsey has a unique relationship with the European Economic Community, being the subject of a special Protocol attached to the United Kingdom's Treaty of Accession to the E.E.C. In general terms this preserves Guernsey's traditional economic links with the United Kingdom and provides for free movement of industrial and agricultural goods to and from the E.E.C., but apart from matters affecting the Island's visible trade it is only very lightly involved with the Community. In particular, Guernsey remains free to determine its own tax structure and is not required to harmonise commercial and most other legislation. Until comparatively recent times the economy of the Island was based mainly on horticulture and tourism, but during the last ten to fifteen years finance centre activities have become a major source of revenue.

Finance Centre Services

Guernsey has established itself as a major international off-shore financial centre, a development which is based on its long history of political stability, proximity to the City of London, and to an ever-lessening extent its position within the Sterling Area.

There are now some 47 banks established in the Island, most of which are branches or subsidiaries of major international banks with head offices in the United Kingdom, Australia, Belgium, Canada, Italy, the Netherlands, the USA and elsewhere. Guernsey is also one of the leading offshore insurance centres in the world, and is the home of many life assurance, reinsurance and captive insurance companies, the latter being "in-house" insurance subsidiaries owned by large commercial or industrial groups to insure their own risks, thereby making substantial savings in their insurance costs. The Island is also well-known as a base for offshore funds, that is unit trusts and unit trust type investment companies.

Legal, Accountancy and Other Services

A number of international firms of accountants have offices in the Island and both they and the local Advocates (lawyers — who must be United Kingdom barristers or solicitors as well as being qualified in Guernsey Law) are well versed in the special requirements of Captives. As well as specialist insurance management companies a full range of ancillary services are available through the local offices of consultant actuaries, stockbrokers, moneybrokers, etc.

Corporation Tax Companies

These are companies which although incorporated in Guernsey do not carry on business in the Island and are controlled and managed elsewhere. Such companies pay Guernsey Corporation Tax, currently £300 p.a. (or Guernsey income tax at 20% on their profits, whichever is the less). Captives have been established in the past as corporation tax companies, but in future all Guernsey incorporated insurance companies will have to be resident in the Island.

But why should this small Island in the English Channel have attained such an important position in the world of international finance?

A major attraction of Guernsey is undoubtedly the low rate of income tax, which for residents is 20% on both personal incomes and business profits, and there are no capital gains taxes, wealth taxes, death duties, sales taxes or V.A.T. Non-residents availing themselves of the investment and other financial facilities which the Island has to offer can normally do so without incurring any liability to Guernsey income tax.

Many small countries with favourable tax regimes for non-residents have not had the success of Guernsey in developing as financial centres. In a troubled and ever changing world, international investors are seeking a safe refuge for their assets. Guernsey inspires confidence as such a refuge because of its long history of independent, stable Government; and financial policies based on the Government balancing its budget year in year out without recourse either to borrowing or increases in income tax. The Island's proximity to the city of London (the Capital is one hour's flying time away), its first-class educational system and the excellence of its telecommunications are other important factors in its success, while visiting businessmen appreciate the high standard of the hotels and restaurants.

The depth of financial expertise which now exists in the Island and the high reputation which it enjoys internationally will ensure that Guernsey remains a leading offshore financial centre in the future.

Taxation Geared for Growth

Guernsey's unusual constitutional independence has allowed it to develop a body of taxation legislation designed to maximise personal and corporate freedom.

Personal and corporate taxes are assessed at a single rate of 20% and there is no distinction between profits retained in the enterprise and distribution to shareholders.

Investment and expansion can be financed from retained earnings to an extent not possible elsewhere, complicated tax codes and regulations are eliminated, and the businessman is free to devote his time to more productive and profitable matters.

As for estate and death duties, gift, wealth, capital gains, sales or value added taxes — they don't exist in Guernsey. And rates on property taxes are consistent with the Island's generally low taxation levels.

Business Profits

Business profits are subject to a conventional income tax of 20%. Profits are computed on ordinary business principles, and there are capital allowances for commercial buildings, plant and machinery. There is no Corporation Tax, such as in the United Kingdom.

Personal Taxation

Income from all sources is aggregated, personal and other allowances are deducted, and the remainder taxed at a flat 20p in the £.

Double Taxation Relief

Guernsey has entered into arrangements for the avoidance of Double Taxation with the United Kingdom and Jersey.

Where doubly taxed income arises in another territory (i.e. not the United Kingdom or Jersey) unilateral relief is given in Guernsey. This relief is given at whichever is the lower of the overseas effective rate or three-quarters of the Guernsey effective rate. Any overseas tax which is not relieved by credit is relieved by deduction from the gross income.

Other Taxes

In Guernsey there is no Capital Gains Tax, no Capital Transfer Tax or Death Duties nor is there a Wealth Tax. The Island does not have to comply with European Economic Community regulations concerning Value Added Tax and therefore there is no Value Added Tax nor any Sales Tax.

Communications and Services

Year-through communications with both UK and the Continent remove any possible doubts one might hold concerning an island location. In fact, a business trip to or from London is faster and more convenient than between London and many UK destinations.

Situated as it is a mere 30 miles from France, Guernsey is an ideal location for trade with the Continent, and regular container and cargo services operate between Guernsey, Cherbourg, St Malo and Rotterdam.

Air Services

Guernsey has direct air services to many British airports and to a number of Continental destinations, including Paris and Amsterdam. Airlines operate several daily services from London's Heathrow and Gatwick airports, and through a rail-air link to the capital via Southampton. In addition, there is a 'bus-stop' air service link with Jersey which extends the number of destinations which can be reached.

There are regular air freight services to Bournemouth and Southend and freight is also carried on scheduled passenger routes. British Airways provides a world wide service from Guernsey.

Sea Services

A fast hydrofoil service operates between Guernsey and the other major Channel Islands and to the French port of St Malo.

Roll-on/Roll-off ferries operate a regular service to Guernsey from Portsmouth, Weymouth, and Cherbourg and there are regular container and cargo services to Portsmouth, St Malo and Rotterdam. Many other ports are serviced by coastal traders. First class port handling and containerisation services operate.

Cultural Life

Together with the natural beauty of the Island comes a civilised, sophisticated life. Concerts, theatre and the arts form an integral part of the Island's leisure. Its restaurants are a gourmet's paradise, and its shops display the best of both English and French goods — at prices often considerably below those prevailing in either country.

Sports

Sports are generously catered for. Naturally, those relating to the sea are predominant — over 10,000 foreign yachts anchor annually in St Peter Port, often described as one of the most attractive harbour capitals in Europe. Windsurfing, fishing, water skiing . . . and, of course, the unequalled facilities for swimming and sunbathing.

Golf, tennis, squash, badminton, cricket, football, rugby, bowls and even softball are represented by a number of clubs, and a multi-million pound all-purpose leisure centre provides facilities for virtually the whole range of sporting activities.

Immigration

The Island's prosperity and high quality of life are reflected in its housing.

Because of population pressures on the Island's limited resources of land and housing, legislation has been introduced to control the occupation of dwellings in Guernsey by persons without residential qualifications. This legislation makes provision for the release of housing licences to persons brought to the Island to fill positions considered to be essential to the well-being of the community.

Licences to occupy local market houses, or houses constructed specifically for the purpose, for essential members of their staff may be applied for provided it can be shown that persons with the requisite skills and expertise are not available in Guernsey and that the enterprise is of benefit to the Island both financially and as an employer of local labour.

For those to whom the Housing Authority cannot justify the release of a housing licence, approximately 10% of the 18,000 dwellings are freely available for purchase and occupation. These 'open market' properties are generally the larger type of dwelling of relatively high cost, whereas the other 90% of houses are 'local market' and are purchased and sold at prices which can be afforded by the permanent population with residential qualifications or housing licences.

THE ISLE OF MAN

Larry Kearns
Shannon Kneale & Co., Chartered Accountants

Offshore financial centres require five basic qualities to ensure their success and these can be summarised as political stability, a suitable tax structure, a stable currency, a good system of communications and transport, and finally a high standard of professional expertise.

The primary requirement of any tax haven is that it operates a suitable taxation structure and that basically it has a low level of direct taxation.

The gradual swing to the left in European politics in the past decade has ensured that wealthy individuals and multi-national corporations have sought to base their operations in areas where the likelihood of communist groups attaining political power is remote. The emergence of black power in the Caribbean has also provoked a number of multi-national businesses into moving their operations away for fear that revolution will put the future of those Islands into jeopardy.

It is obviously a pre-requisite of any tax haven that the currency used by the financial centre is stable and not subject to violent fluctuation, as there is little point in minimising tax liabilities if the potential fall in the value of the currency outweighs any tax saving.

Financial centres require a high standard of telecommunications in order that professional decisions which can be concluded in any part of the world can be relayed to the relevant jurisdiction in as quick a time as possible. Similarly high standards and frequency of transport are required.

It is apparent that no financial centre can survive unless the standards of its professional people are very high. Wealthy corporations and individuals are unwilling to entrust their affairs to people who are inexperienced or unable to carry out their requirements.

European Requirements

The development of financial centres over the past decade has resulted in a number of the original centres consolidating their position, and a number of other islands entering into the field of low tax areas. Offshore financial centres tend to grow up in geographical proximity to the wealthy countries and more dynamic economies of the world.

This is evidenced by the fact that in the Far East, Singapore and Hong Kong have grown up as major offshore financial centres; in the Middle East, Cyprus has developed similarly; in America, the Caribbean islands and Bermuda have tended to be used more frequently as low tax areas to service the requirements of American corporations and individuals.

Similarly in Europe, Liechtenstein, Switzerland, Luxembourg and a number of other low tax jurisdictions have grown up to service European requirements. Great Britain has seen the development of Jersey, Guernsey and the Isle of Man to a degree, as offshore financial centres which sought to cater for the needs of British residents.

As a result of this it is generally accepted that our primary competitors at this moment in this field are Jersey, Guernsey, and possibly Gibraltar. It cannot be denied that Jersey and Guernsey are better known financial centres than the Isle of Man and that they presently provide a wider range of services to a greater market than the Isle of Man does. Both areas offer all the requirements I have mentioned above and have now acquired a degree of respectability. The financial infrastructure on both of these Islands is more sophisticated than that existing in the Isle of Man although we are rapidly catching up.

This is evidenced by the number of international banks, accountants, legal and other financial advisers that presently operate out of those Islands.

International Market

The development of Jersey and Guernsey on an international basis over the last few years has also made the Manx Government realise that if it is to compete it must look beyond the shores of Great Britain and appeal to the international market.

The advantages offered by all three islands are broadly the same and the structures most frequently used are the Trust and non-resident company.

Manx non-resident companies are frequently used in preference to Jersey non-resident companies because there is no requirement to divulge the name of the beneficial owner of the company to the Manx authorities as there is in Jersey.

Freeport

The Exempt Insurance Companies Act of 1981 (soon to be superceded by the Insurance Bill 1986) and the introduction of the Exempt Companies Bill 1984 offer further advantages over the Channel Islands in the captive insurance and shipping management fields. A Freeport has also been established in an effort to attract light industry to the Isle of Man and exploit one great advantage the Island has over the Channel Islands in the fact that it is not so densely populated and readily welcomes light industry and new residents to its shores.

The Isle of Man is still in its formative years as an offshore financial centre and unlike Jersey it has not closed its doors to international banks and has adequate space for development to house the individuals who will work in the new financial institutions.

The fact that the Isle of Man is less well developed financially has also resulted in services on the Island tending to be significantly cheaper than in the Channel Islands.

Right Scenario

Now that the problems in the banking sector have been tackled and the Financial Supervision Commission has taken its place on the Isle of Man it is reasonable to assume that the problems that have arisen in the past will not recur.

Having set the right scenario and proved that proper facilities exist on the Isle of Man at a reasonable price, it is now imperative that the advantages of the Isle of Man are brought home to the international market and attempts are currently being made at both Government and business levels to ensure that the benefits of the Isle of Man are known to the world.

This is not an easy task and will require a concerted effort over a period of time. For this reason the arrivals of banks, firms of accountants, lawyers and other advisers of international status should be welcomed as through their own international links they can spread the word of the benefits of the Island to a far wider audience and bring work to the Island that would traditionally have gone elsewhere.

Immigration

In February 1985, Tynwald, the Isle of Man's long-established Parliament, decided to make it clear to the world that there is a positive welcome waiting for those who would like to live on the Island.

A question that has been frequently asked since this policy was made public is "Why should you wish to increase the population size?" The simple answer is that there is ample room for expansion on the Island, with a population of less than 65,000 living on 572 square kilometres (221 square miles), the population density is some 6 or 7 times less that that in the Channel Islands. Also, Tynwald prides itself in the quality of its health, education and social services and it is clear that these services could cope readily with an increase in population of 10,000. In fact many services, particularly electricity supply and other public utilities, benefit greatly from an increase in the number of consumers. Furthermore, the various amenities provided for tourists require a strong domestic market to thrive and increased consumption by residents will improve the standard of retailing and restaurants available for visitors. In addition, the recreational facilities, such as golf, sailing, rambling and fishing, have substantial spare capacity to cater for additional demand.

The policy to attract new residents is seen to be complementary to the programme of economic development that has now been followed for a number of years. The aim of the development programme is to encourage greater income and employment opportunities for the Manx population. The paradox is that even without the effect of immigration, increasing numbers of school leavers will raise the size of the working population in the next few years, whereas the retired population will decline in size. However, although there is a growing pool of labour available on the Island, it is necessary to attract a range of other people who are able to stimulate economic activity in some way.

"What type of people are you trying to attract?" is another question often asked. Essentially the policy is designed to encourage those who will integrate well into Manx society and who, one way or another, will make a contribution to the Island's economic well-being.

Research into the reasons which people have for being interested in moving to the Isle of Man has shown that it is a combination of factors that is found to be attractive. A better life style, scenic beauty and peacefulness, friendliness of the people, the stability of Tynwald with its non-party Members and over 1,000 years of independent rule, the low crime rate, the low property rates, low taxation (20% maximum on the earnings of both companies and individuals) and absence of wealth, capital gains and death duties, are all factors which figure frequently in the comments of those considering a move to the Isle of Man.

Thus, the type of individual who may wish to establish his business or his home in the Island and who will be made welcome, may have a variety of different profiles. The active businessman may wish to establish his business in a place which is attractive as a location for industry and yet which also provides himself and his family with a pleasant lifestyle. Generally, this man will be attracted by the range of financial incentives and the taxation advantages which are available both to his company and himself. Usually he is surprised to find that the Island already has over 200 manufacturing companies and the tradition of engineering. (Manufacturing is second only to Finance as a source of national income). The fact that the Island finances all its own services and makes a contribution to the United Kingdom for defence and diplomatic services generally interests the new resident as does the Island's unique constitutional position with both the European Community and the United Kingdom. The fact that the Isle of Man is not, and never has been, a part of the United Kingdom is not widely known and whereas there are extremely strong emotional, economic and cultural links with the United Kingdom, Tynwald is proud of its ability to legislate for all internal matters. This ensures that appropriate fiscal policies can be formulated and means that Tynwald can act in a way which most benefits the local population. The principle underlying most policies is that business activity flourishes best when not hampered by bureaucracy. The role of Government is seen to be one of creating the right environment in which the private sector can prosper so that the wealth generated will have beneficial effects throughout the economy.

The Island's relationship with the European Community, a market of over 300 million people, is also interesting. The Isle of Man is not a member of the European Community but has a "special relationship" as a result of Protocol 3 to the United Kingdom's Treaty of Accession. This "special relationship" guarantees traders in the Isle of Man free trade with the rest of the Community as the Island is deemed to lie within the external tariff barriers. However, there is no involvement whatsoever with the Community's budget, the Island neither contributes to, nor receives any assistance from, Community funds. Also, the Island is not involved with the long-term objectives of harmonisation of tax, employment and social legislation. This means that the Island is able to enjoy the benefits of free trade with the Community while avoiding the restrictions that often result from membership of such a large, heterogeneous organisation.

Typically, the prospective new resident wishing to establish his home and business in the Isle of Man will expect costs to be high and labour to be difficult to employ. In reality the labour force is renowned for its loyalty and stability and the size of the industrial sector, employing some 13% of the employed population, coupled with extensive Government schemes for training and retraining, means that incoming companies are usually well-pleased with the labour available. Also Government tries hard to balance the need to protect the workforce from the hardship of redundancy with the need to ensure that regulations are not so onerous that they discourage firms from developing. There is a system of work permits which is designed to encourage companies to employ local labour when this is available, but where skills are in short supply then permits are readily supplied. Financial assistance is available in a variety of forms with grants of up to 40%, marketing and training allowances and 100% writing down allowances being made available to suitable applicants.

Studies of the cost of living compared with that in the United Kingdom indicate that across-the-board costs are more or less identical. However, in certain areas such as energy and transport, there are additional costs associated with the geographical situation of being an island with a relatively low population. This means that firms best suited to the Isle of Man are those with reasonable energy requirements and with a relatively high value but low bulk output. Compensating these higher costs are the costs of housing, which are over 26% less than the average in the United Kingdom. Office and industrial building costs are also relatively much lower, particularly when account is taken of the insignificant rates which are levied. For example, a modern 10,000 square foot factory near Douglas, the capital and main centre of population, would be charged some £500 per annum.

In addition to the businessman who may wish to establish a company on the Island, the small firm employing as few as 5-10 people is made particularly welcome, the Isle of Man welcomes other categories of new resident.

The expatriate or retired person wishing simply to reside on the Island may find the position relating to taxation, especially the absence of capital taxes, to be of interest and the sophisticated financial sector is always ready to provide advice on investments. Also, there are jobs available for skilled engineering craftsmen who may wish to move to a community which is able to provide security and a quality way of life for his family.

Another question that is often asked is "What are the entry restrictions?" The answer is simple. Provided that the prospective new resident has full permanent residency rights in the United Kingdom or Irish Republic there is complete freedom of entry and abode. Naturally, immigration regulations are more involved for those with different citizenship, but every effort is made to ensure that people are acquainted with the particular regulations which may affect them. Overseas nationals can obtain full details and immigration application forms from their nearest British Embassy or Consulate which represent the Island in such matters. It is important to stress that the Isle of Man is keen to attract all those new residents who would be compatible with the relaxed way of life enjoyed on the Island and who would make a contribution, in terms of their skills or their spending power, to the Manx economy.

Finally, it is reasonable to ask why the Isle of Man is not inundated with people if the quality of life and financial attractions are as outstanding as suggested in this article. Once again, the answer is straight forward. Until now the Isle of Man has made little effort to market its attributes and it is very common to hear outsiders express surprise at the range of features they find on the Island. Government now recognises the need to announce to the world that new residents are welcome to the Isle of Man and has embarked on a policy to expand the population in conjunction with the continued development of banking, financial and insurance services and manufacturing. At the same time the tourist industry is being restructured into a sophisticated leisure industry which will complement the new resident policy. Also, the nurturing of new services based on the management of merchant shipping, with Island-based staff operating within the new merchant shipping regulations, has produced a thriving new growth sector.

Thus, the new residents policy is designed to complement the other facets of economic policy, the overall aim being to generate income and employment.

CARING CARNATIONS

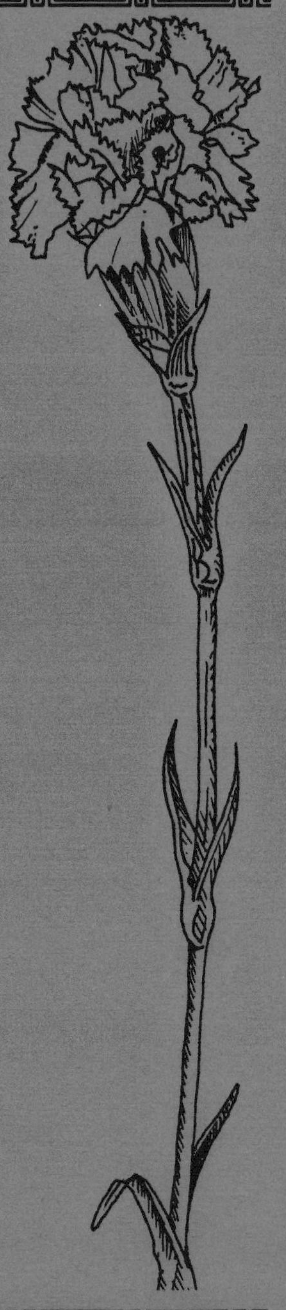

Jersey is famous for its ability to provide top quality carnations all the year round. Picked at exactly the right moment and carefully packed to ensure that they arrive in perfect condition, thirty of these first class blooms will be carefully boxed and airmailed to the UK mainland to provide the ideal birthday or anniversary gift, Mother's Day, Easter, or Christmas present or a simply superb "I love you" reminder to someone special in your life and from who you are now far away.

EXPATXTRA!, as part of its services to the world-wide working British expatriate community has made exclusive arrangements with Jersey's leading carnation specialists to provide this Caring Carnation service. All you have to do is tell us to whom the flowers should be sent, the date by which they should arrive and we will do the rest. Provided, of course, that you also send us a cheque in payment! Don't worry if you cannot find locally a suitable card to enclose with the flowers; we will inscribe your message on any one of a selection of carefully chosen greeting cards for you.

Send us your name and address, the name and address of the recipient-to-be, the occasion being celebrated, the date for delivery and your message, a cheque for £15.00 [made payable to EXPATXTRA!] per order and we shall do the rest.

Why! we can even deal with multiple orders; you can stop worrying whether you will forget that special anniversary, Mother's Day or whatever and send us a list of the names and addresses, dates of the special days, the messages you wish to have enclosed, cheque to cover the cost and leave the rest to us. We haven't failed to deliver the goods yet; as expatriates in over 100 countries of the world will tell you.

Write [BLOCK CAPITALS FOR NAMES, ADDRESSES AND MESSAGES PLEASE] to Caring Carnations, EXPATXTRA!, PO Box 300, Jersey, Channel Islands; enclose your name and address [just in case we have any difficulty and wish to confirm your delivery instructions], the names and addresses of the recipients, the delivery dates, the occasions being celebrated, the messages to be enclosed, and a cheque covering the cost of each order of thirty carnations [£15 each including packing and airmail post, made payable to EXPATXTRA!] and we shall see that your delivery instructions are carried out to the petal!

JERSEY

Jersey is the most southerly and biggest of the Channel Islands, 45 square miles in area with a population of some 76,000.

In a world of continuing political instability Jersey stands out like a refuge. The States of Jersey, the Island's parliament, comprises 53 members all of whom are elected as individuals and not as members of any political party. In domestic matters the Island has complete autonomy but through the Island's allegiance to the British Crown, Her Majesty's Government is responsible for Jersey's international affairs.

As with the other Channel Islands the constitutional relationship between Jersey and the United Kingdom is unwritten but founded on custom and usage over nine centuries; for this reason it can be considered to be far stronger than something more formal but more recent, that is the product of political negotiation.

Fiscal independence

The Island's allegiance to the Crown was rewarded in times long past by the granting of charters by the English monarchs that established two of the most important features of the Island's economic life to-day; the free trade relationship with the UK and the fiscal independence it enjoys.

Upon the Island's fiscal independence and its political stability has been founded the present low tax status and the maintenance of that status. The minimum and standard rate of tax on all income, both personal and corporate, is twenty per cent. The absence of any capital taxation or value added tax, and the low rates of duty which apply to alcoholic drink, tobacco, petrol and perfume are not the result of political manipulation of recent years designed to attract and capture for the Island a share of the world's business looking for a low tax refuge or holidaymakers looking for inexpensive holidays. They arise from stable, conservative government pursuing a policy of prudent budgeting with a strong attachment to the principle — not very evident elsewhere in the world — that governments should spend the money they know they have and not borrow in anticipation of what they might have in the future. Suggest to any member of the Island's government or civil service that Jersey is a "tax haven" and you are likely to receive short shrift. The Island's present Lieutenant-Governor, Sir William Pillar, is on record as saying "I feel a little aggrieved when I hear Jersey referred to as a "tax haven." This implies that the rate of tax is held at a deliberately low rate in order to attract the rich immigrant or the funds of expatriates, rather than being the level at which sufficient revenue is generated to meet the Island's needs. It is an unfair description of a lovely, well run Island". Jersey's rate of income tax has remained the same for over 40 years.

Economic prosperity

The commitment of Jersey to retain the Island's low-tax status upon which

Picking a path to profitable investment
What you want out of life now, and later, depends on your making the right choice today!
There are as many reasons for investing as there are investors and a great variety of things to invest in — unit trusts, stocks and shares, property, bank accounts and insurance to name a few.
These days, the successful investor needs to be sure footed and have a full team looking after his investments on a full time basis.
The Britannia team is currently responsible for the management of over £4,000m (US$5,800m) for more than 350,000 investors through it's network of offices worldwide.
But take one decisive step now! Complete and post the coupon below and we will tell you how the Britannia team can help you find the path to profitable investment.
To: Douglas D. Aitken
Britannia International Investment Management Limited
P.O. Box 271, St. Helier, Jersey, Channel Islands
1. Do you require Income or capital growth
2. Would you invest: Regularly and/or lump sum
3. How long do you anticipate maintaining your investment.
1—2 years 2—3 years 3—5 years + 5 years
4. Would you prefer to invest in Sterling or U.S. Dollars
Name (in capitals)
Address
WAEE
Tel. No.
All enquiries will be treated in the strictest confidence
Britannia
INTERNATIONAL
INVESTMENT MANAGEMENT
LIMITED
P.O. Box 271, Queensway House, Queen Street, St. Helier, Jersey, Channel Islands.
Tel: Jersey (0534) 73114 Telex: 4192092
A member of the Britannia Arrow Group
International Financial Services

economic prosperity has been built, is best reflected in the response of the States to the decision of the UK Government to join the EEC. The policy of fiscal harmonisation enshrined in the Treaty of Rome and the administrative burden inherent in the application of many directives and regulations constantly emanating from Brussels, were not attractive to the Island. Jersey was successful, with the aid of the UK Government, in negotiating a relationship with the EEC that can best be described as an extension to the EEC of the connections which have for a long time existed with the United Kingdom. So it is that the Island retains autonomy in domestic matters and, even more important, fiscal policy, but is party to the Community's free trade regime in agricultural and manufactured goods.

Almost coincidental with the setting up of this relationship with the member states of the EEC came the Island's own economic policies directed at making Jersey an international offshore centre. The Island is in monetary union with the UK and therefore shares both the strengths and the weaknesses of sterling and the fluctuations in UK interest rates.

Jersey, the financial centre

Up to the early 1960s Jersey's economy was largely dependent on tourists drawn from the United Kingdom. During that decade the Island began to develop as a financial centre; largely as a refuge for the funds of foreigners and non-residents of the UK who wished to have or needed to have funds within the sterling area but also wished to enjoy freedom from high UK taxation.

Thus Jersey's pre-eminent role as one of the financial centres for international finance was born.

Tourism remains an important contributor to the Island's national income; it accounts for almost a third of it. Nearly eighty per cent of the visitors [765,000 of them spent £175 million in 1984] come from the UK but increasingly Dutch, German and Scandinavian languages are to be heard along Jersey's wide shopping precincts, merging with the more usual French from our close neighbours on the continental mainland.

But the real growth sector of the past decade has been the finance centre activities which now account for approximately 30 per cent of Jersey's national income. In 1973 deposits held by banks on the Island totalled £1 billion; now-a-days the figure has increased beyond £24 billion, much of which is in foreign currencies. In 1973 there were 306 investment and trading companies formed by residents outside the British Isles; that figure rose to over 1800 in 1984.

Additionally many companies registered elsewhere by non-residents are being administered by Jersey's lawyers [advocates], accountants and trust company administrators and banks; services all used because of the high standard of professionalism and expertise they offer.

There were over £2.5 billion under administration by a wide range of investment managers on the Island in mid-1985.

This growth has occurred due largely to the decision, early in the Island's development as a financial centre, to pursue all practical steps to build up a reputation for service and respectability. The Island resisted the temptation to grow faster without taking sufficient regard for the source of the business, or the standing of the insitutions involved. The objective the Island set itself was to secure a sound reputation as a respectable, stable, professionally competent low tax area.

This objective has been achieved, the reputation has been established and now the Island is in the position of not being able [or willing?] to accommodate many businesses which would wish to enjoy this "*paradis fiscaux*".

This policy is no better reflected than in the Island's banking community. Jersey has not sought to compete with other low tax areas in the number of banks registered; rather it has concentrated on quality. Of the 52 deposit taking institutions registered under Jersey's Depositor and Investors law [which excludes the branch offices in the Island of the London Clearing Banks and the Trustee Savings Bank of the Channel Islands] 41 are related to banks in the world's top 500 and 48 are related to banks that have a presence in London holding recognised bank status under the UK Banking Act.

By this means Jersey has avoided the difficulties that many other offshore centres, and those depositing funds in those centres, have experienced.

No tax is levied in Jersey on the interest from deposits made by non-residents of the Island nor on capital gains accrued by investment through the many excellent investment fund managers practising within its shores. Thus it is that, along with its policy of allowing only the best to practise their skills here, Jersey has built itself into a financial centre admired throughout the world.

A similar approach has been adopted in respect to institutions managing offshore funds as is made to banks. The proclaimed view of the Island is that institutions of stature will protect the good name of the Island because they themselves have a good name to protect.

It cannot be said that the Island is without its problems; the major one is that the Island is small and rightly wishes to preserve an environment and quality of life that is increasingly difficult to find elsewhere. So it cannot, for a start, accommodate everyone who would wish to come and live here.

The Island is virtually unique; at a time when most countries are troubled by high unemployment and are searching for ways to increase economic activity, Jersey has pretty near full employment and has had to introduce regulations for limiting the rate of business growth and immigration.

Immigration

Only such businesses that will enhance the reputation of the Island are allowed to set up a physical presence here; and even then provided that they do not make too

heavy demands on the need to house immigrant staff. Such limitations do not apply to non-residents wanting to set up companies or trusts here to take advantage of the low tax facilities; just to those who seek to come and work in Jersey and thus increase the pressure on housing and other facilities.

Jersey's aim is to hold the Island's population below 80,000; the immigration laws are designed to achieve that aim.

Residence here is restricted to those who take up essential employment and those who can satisfy the authorities that their presence in the Island will be of substantial economic or social benefit; one of the criteria is that immigrants in the latter category should contribute also to the Island's tax coffers quite substantially. Consents for wealthy immigrants to Jersey are currently limited to around 15 a year, require the purchase of a house in excess of [about] £250,000 and the proof of a Jersey taxable income considerably in excess of £50,000.

As one of my colleagues remarked "It may well be easier for a rich man to enter the Kingdom of Heaven than appease the Jersey immigration department".

So expatriates wishing to come to live here after amassing their fortunes abroad will have had to amass sizeable ones and be one of the 15 or so lucky immigrants a year who can show cause and means sufficient to pass the requirements.

Expatriates who have ambitions of a lesser kind but ambitions which involve a proper approach to their future financial well-being should not overlook the huge advantages of banking here, using the services of investment managers here, and obtaining professional counselling from the accountants, advocates and other advisers skilled and experienced in expatriate affairs.

RETURNING HOME

NOW HE IS TREADING THAT DARK ROAD TO THE PLACE NO ONE HAS EVER RETURNED
HOME

Expatriates, whether long term or short term, practically always discover that during their time abroad mistakes have been made which they would not like to repeat; yet often the mistakes are compounded due to lack of forethought.

In the tax chapter I have already outlined the tax consequences that can befall an expatriate who returns to the UK rather more swiftly than he intended.

If you have made a meal out of this book by reading it chapter by chapter [rather than picking at it, like a "faddy" eater] you will expect, no doubt, that in this chapter I shall be issuing dire warnings. You might well expect that this chapter, the last in the book, will be full of cautions; that should you not heed the advice it contains the worse it will be for you.

I will not disappoint you! But in the main they will be cautions about matters which have been explored elsewhere in the book; let that not put you off reading this chapter, please.

UK tax consequences to be considered

I have already stressed in the tax chapter the fact that, all too often, working expatriates overlook the ramifications of an unscheduled visit during the life of their overseas contract of employment. Many are unaware, through ignorance or innocence, of the pitfalls; just as many, through stupidity or sheer arrogance, disregard them.

"How does the Inland Revenue know that I, or my wife, ever visited the UK?" expatriates have asked me; adding smugly, "after all my passport isn't stamped any more".

The plain fact is that the Inland Revenue are normally unaware of short, interim visits paid by expatriates or their families to the UK during their period abroad. Passports are no longer stamped by UK immigration officers; no dates of entry or exit into or from the UK appear in that black covered, cardboard billet doux which Her Britannic Majesty's Principal Secretary of State for Foreign and Commonwealth Affairs allows us to carry around the world and which requests and requires all those damned foreigners to allow us to pass freely without let or hindrance through their borders having afforded us all the help and protection as may be necessary. Those of us who queue regularly to enter the United States of America at Los Angeles airport might wonder, during the course of the three days we are in the line, whether any of them can read, or, if they can, whether they ever take any notice.

No; there is no official UK record of comings and goings but he who makes the statement begs the question.

If you are one of those who hold dear the doctrine that "what the Inland Revenue does not know does no harm" you will not mind my enquiring "how does the Revenue know that you have been working abroad and not moonlighting in a pub in Macclesfield for a couple of years or more?"

Undoubtedly your answer will be "because I haven't; I **have** been working abroad".

At which I — better I than the Inland Revenue surely — will say "prove it!"

Remember that it is the statutory duty of any UK national to account to the

Inland Revenue for any tax liablility that he may have, or even thinks that he might have.

The Inland Revenue's role in the relationship is in two parts; the first is to establish on the evidence presented to determine that the quantum of assessed tax is correct and the second is to collect it.

If told a pack of falsehoods the Revenue may well believe what they are told; or they may question the information they have been given.

Statements made to the Inland Revenue are made under a declaration that they are true; tell "fibs" and you will run the risk of being discovered to be telling fibs. The consequences can, to say the least, be unpleasant. Having determined the fact that you owe them some tax the Revenue will seek to perform their second function with enormous vigour. Leaving it up to you, the intending tax evader perhaps, to prove them wrong — if you can.

I have to admit that I could be accused of overstating a case; that I am lumping together the sheep with the goats. But that, surely, is the way of things in this imperfect world. A great deal of anti-avoidance legislation, enacted by the UK Parliament at the behest of the Inland Revenue would never have been necessary were it not for the fact that someone — not you or I, of course — had attempted to "pull a fast one".

As a result people who wished to fund their children's school fees via certain types of life assurance policies have been prevented from doing so; people who wished to set up small companies and receive UK Government grants have had their abilities to do so curtailed; simply because others took totally unfair advantage of a piece of legislation designed to be of use to the modest investor. The good expatriates who quite carefully try to stay within the rules would find less restricting UK tax legislation barring their road to financial happiness if it were not for the attitudes and actions of the occasional "naughty" expatriate.

The payment of taxes in the UK by any expatriate is, to a great extent, dependent upon his honesty [or otherwise]. I have heard of ingenious schemes to avoid UK tax; schemes dreamed up by expatriates who think that they have nothing better to do but devise wangles.

I, for one, have too great a respect for the Investigation Department of the Inland Revenue to suggest to any expatriate that he should test the taxman's ingenuity to counteract any such arrangements.

The three areas of greatest concern that ought be uppermost in every working expatriate's mind is not how to evade tax [totally illegal] but how to get himself and his family into a position where tax is avoided or mitigated [not illegal]. Generally the concern [as well as the tax impositions] can be lessened by

a] avoiding breaking the rules set out in the Finance Act 1977 and/or abiding by the regulations which determine non-residence

b] ensuring that, if returning to the UK [for however short a period] at a

time when not in full time employment abroad [between contracts?], no "accommodation" is available for your use

c] a modicum of pre-planning if returning to the UK to assume tax residence.

These three matters are so important that, despite the fact that I have stressed them previously, I shall do so again.

The one sixth rule — Finance Act 1977

Every recent British expatriate needs to pass through a period of working overseas during which time he is vulnerable to the incursions of this legislation. Every working British expatriate without exception who has left the shores of the UK since April 1977 has had to do so. If he has not managed to pass through the vulnerability period successfully then a tax liability will have resulted.

In order to become not resident and not ordinarily resident for UK tax purposes every expatriate must work abroad in full time and continuous employment for a period which incorporates a full fiscal year, must not visit the UK for more than 90 days on average year after year [and less than 183 days in any one tax year] and perform all the duties of his employment [other than incidental duties] outside the UK.

If an expatriate cannot claim to have fulfilled those requirements he is forced back into the shelter of the "one sixth rule". He has to calculate his total qualifying days and, hopefully, succeed in his claim to receive the 100 per cent deduction. To do so he would need to prove his whereabouts; need categorically to be able to prove in which days he was in which country and — in some cases — at what hour of the day he arrived in the UK. And, to quote the immortal words of thousands of expatriates, his passport isn't stamped!

So as much "evidence" as you can muster as to your movements across the face of the globe will be helpful if you are challenged to prove your claim to the 100 per cent deduction; air tickets, hotel bills, restaurant receipts etc.

It may sound far fetched but in mid-May 1986 I was involved in a situation whereby an expatriate who had been abroad for only 370 days was able to prove that he was in Qatar on a particular day in question by producing an American Express counterfoil. The charge card showed an expenditure of £35.00; the potential liability to UK tax was just short of £17,000. When shown the receipted counterfoil the tax inspector missed the golden opportunity to smile and say "that will do nicely, thank you".

Incidental duties

I have explained elsewhere how important it is for any expatriate to watch the substance of any duties which he performs within the UK: any expatriate who is intent on reaping the benefits from being a non-resident for UK tax purposes, that is. I have also repeated, verbatim, the Revenue's warning about the fact that they consider it hardly likely that any duties performed by a **Director of an overseas**

company will ever be regarded as "merely incidental" to the overseas duties. I do not intend to explore that point further; only to re-emphasise it since it is a matter often over looked and rarely commented upon.

The last time I published an edition of this book I received nearly one hundred letters from readers around the world asking me, in confidence, whether I thought that some duty that they had performed [in some instances, regularly performed on an on-going basis] would escape the Revenue's wrath. In the end I had two letters duplicated; one which I sent to those who told me they held directorships, the other to those who did not. In both letters I had to point out that I was not the arbiter in such matters; but that taking the Revenue's statements as an indication of their intentions

i] no duties of a director was likely to be considered incidental

ii] a sales manager employed by a Hong Kong firm was really chancing his arm if he went to the UK to sell his equipment

iii] as was the personnel manager of an Arab conglomerate who interviewed prospective staff at a hotel in the UK [four times a year for a fortnight at a time!] and

iv] an accountant employed in Nigeria who regularly went back to Scotland to attend the "in house" audit of the group of companies for whom he worked abroad should know better.

As I have also previously stressed the movements in and out the UK by the non-working spouse of a working expatriate can also determine whether or not the financial well-being of the family remains unadulterated by a succession of buff envelopes from the Revenue.

I have long since given up counting the number of words that I write on expatriate matters each year; too many, some would say and there are times, were I honest about it, when I would echo their assessment.

Particularly when a considerable number of the words repeats and repeats the message that non-working expatriates must not have accommodation available to them during visits to the UK should they aspire to becoming or remaining non-resident.

The available accommodation rule is not harsh; just common sense. It is not hard to understand either; surely anyone can tell whether or not he [more likely "she"] has accommodation available. Provided that a room or two in a relative or friend's house is occupied on an "ad hoc" basis during a leave period that is fine; not in contravention of the rules. But it is not fine if you stay with friends or relatives when you could have stayed in your own home.

If you chose to stay in a hotel rather than in your **available** home that is not fine either. In order to comply with the requirements you must not visit the UK at a time when accommodation is available to you if you want to remain a non-resident; never! Unless you are a working expatriate in full time employment abroad; in which case this rule is waived. **Self employed expatriates must be very careful of the "available accommodation" rule.**

So you can see that if you return to the UK at the end of your current contract either to enjoy a period of terminal leave or to attend an interview for another job overseas you will be regarded as resident if at the time you have accommodation available.

Terminal leave

Many employers [particularly UK employers] grant returning expatriates a measure of terminal leave for which they continue paying salary at the overseas rate even if the expatriate chooses to spend his leave within the UK.

If, at the time of his return from overseas employment, he has accommodation available to him within the UK then, from the moment he lands in the UK he will be regarded as resident there for tax purposes. **However, by concession, the Revenue will not seek to charge tax on the salary being paid to him for the month or six weeks leave that he has been allocated.**

If when he returns to the UK his property is occupied by tenants he may still be regarded as resident within the UK; it will depend upon his circumstances and intentions. If he intends to resume duties in the UK then he will be categorised as both resident and ordinarily resident there from the day he returns.

Bonuses or terminal payments made at the end of a successful contract will not be subjected to UK tax even if they are paid in the UK to a person, who has resumed tax residence. Even if, for some reason, the payment is delayed. Often [Nigeria is a prime example] a foreign country has to impose exchange control regulations which inhibit the speedy transfer of terminal payments for several months.

Provided these payments relate to the emoluments of a job performed wholly abroad during a time in which the expatriate was not resident and not ordinarily resident no UK tax will be charged. Naturally the same applies to any savings made from excess overseas income the remittance of which is delayed for some reason. Remember though, if those savings are earning interest then that interest is assessable for UK tax.

Job hunting

Many expatriates, especially professionals such as engineers of all persuasions and others with construction or electrical skills, go abroad to work for a specific contract at the end of which they have to seek further employment either at home or, having got the taste for it, abroad again.

A condition which is a sort of delayed reaction of the symptoms of "expatriatitis", which I described in the Investment and Banking chapter, often sets in. It is a condition far more noticeable to observers and usually totally ignored by the

expatriate suffering from it. It is technically known as "*bravado expatriatitis extremis*"; known to the layman as "cock-suredness".

The effects of this latent symptom are several-fold; the sufferer usually sports a sun tan, a gold Rolex, and a considerable degree of arrogance. He suffers from the delusion that he is very important and that employers will be clamouring for his services.

It can take as long as the major form of expatriatitis to wear off and the period during which these symptoms last are no where near as interesting for the sufferer since he is now spending money on posting unanswered letters begging for a job [any job], train fares to attend abortive interviews, food, mortgage repayments and, probably, expensive school fees for his children. The symptoms can last for many years during which the sufferer gets weaker and weaker, loses his sun tan and his Rolex and becomes more human.

"*Bravado expatriatitis extremis*" can be avoided and is best avoided.

The best preventative is to start looking for a new job about six months prior to the end of the current contract; that will mean having a proper CV prepared, engaging a competent employment consultant and being categoric in your information to him. You should describe in some detail what your requirements would be if only he were super-human and what [considering that he is not] you will accept and when you will be free to accept what he finds.

You should be categoric!

In researching this section of this chapter I discussed the situation with one well known consultant in this field. He showed me [carefully shielding the name of the writers] several letters from expatriates.

His correspondents simply implied that they would be free on such and such a date and would be ready to accept another engagement. No indication of what they thought they could be employed as; where they thought they might like to be employed and what reasonable amount of money they would accept for the new assignment. They failed to indicate whether they were married, had children, required accompanied status jobs or wanted to return to the UK.

I was not surprised when, having shown me the letters, he returned them to a three inch thick file marked "Dead".

So if you require to keep your hopes alive and you do not have another job to which to move once your present contract is over remember the pains of this all too frequent symptom of expatriatitis and make plans to avoid it. It can, as I say, be done and the cure is much the same as the cure for the incipient signs of the problem; get a grip of yourself and give yourself a good talking to.

At all costs try to avoid the trap of returning temporarily to the UK between contracts and falling foul of the available accommodation ruling.

I have already explained that very often the breaching of this rule means that one spouse is resident in the UK whilst the other [usually the husband] can be regarded as not resident.

Although in certain circumstances [that do not affect many working expatriates] that can be an advantage it is, to the majority, a major disadvantage since the couple cannot tax-efficiently share interest bearing bank accounts or investments which might, in the sole hands of the husband, be totally exempt from capital gains tax.

I mentioned in the tax chapter that a recent tax case had determined that the Revenue had been incorrect in their assertion that for capital gains tax purposes spouses could not be considered as "living together" if one were resident and the other non-resident. I explained that in the ***Gubay v Kington*** ruling the Revenue's views had been overturned; but that did not mean that there were not ramifications which ought be most carefully considered [under professional guidance] before being put in train.

Additionally, as I have pointed out, the resident spouse will have to declare to the Revenue the share of the interest allocated from jointly held deposit accounts. As was said in the tax chapter a couple in this predicament has either to accept the tax consequences or forego the pleasure of sharing the account.

Deposit account interest

UK deposit account interest from building societies or UK banks is not subject to income tax in the hands of a non-resident; the Revenue's concession under which such interest is not assessed for tax would be breached if a couple with mixed residential and non residential status were the account holders. In fact, since a resident is taxed on world wide income it would not matter where the account were held; half the interest would be taxable in the resident partner's hands.

For a non-resident **the concession is withdrawn in the year of permanent return** since part of that tax year contains a period of tax residence. **The UK regulations which permit banks and now building societies to pay interest gross to people "not ordinarily resident" for UK tax purposes do not apply during a year in any part of which the account holder is resident in the UK.**

UK account interest

6/4/87	**31/3/88 Permanent return**	**5/4/88**
interest taxable throughout the whole year		

This diagram shows that although the expatriate concerned returned to resume residence very late in the tax year 1987-88 he suffers UK tax on the interest earned on a UK deposit account from the previous 6th April; the start of the tax year.

Had the account been held in the Channel Islands or the Isle of Man UK tax would have been assessable on the interest after his return but not in the period before his repatriation.

Simply by instructing his offshore bankers to cease the foreign source of income [ie to "capitalise interest accrued] to coincide with the day before his return the expatriate would have saved a considerable amount of tax quite legally.

Offshore deposit account interest

6/4/87		31/3/88	5/4/88
	Interest free of any tax	Permanent return New interest taxable in UK	

None of the Channel Islands nor the Isle of Man assess for its income tax requirements interest accrued within its shores by persons not resident there.

Once again I must point out that self employed expatriates, particularly those returning to the UK to enter self employment there, have to be very carefully and specifically advised since in many instances their UK tax liability will be determined on a "previous year" basis. Such expatriates could find that it is to their disadvantage to keep bank accounts offshore of the UK in the final year of their expatriation.

Off-shore investment income should also be taken into account; not just by self employed expatriates but by all working expatriates returning to the UK to resume tax residence.

Remember that some investments held off-shore of the UK will also produce income, albeit by design on many occasions, very little.

If such investments are not disposed of prior to permanent return to the UK then the income received from them [even if re-invested] is subject to UK tax once residence there is resumed.

Capital Gains Tax

CGT will also be charged on any investments held anywhere in the world which are realised for a profit once tax residence is resumed. In fact, unless the expatriate has been regarded as not resident for more than thirty six months, any assets realised at a profit within the year of his return and prior to the date of his return will be assessable too.

It is only those expatriates who have been working abroad for longer than thirty six months who can leave until the last day [almost!] any decision about taking capital gains free of UK CGT.

CGT is charged at 30% [a penny more than the current base rate of UK income tax] so it is a sizeable consideration; but do not take too lightly any decision to sell and avoid CGT. Consult your advisers first. A share or a block of units in a managed fund might be showing a substantial profit; it may be the opinion of your advisers that a peak has yet to be reached.

Selling might save tax but it might also be the wrong move as far as future profits are concerned.

You should consider **"bed and breakfast"** techniques. By this means you arrange to sell the assets one day and buy them back the next. Thus you can establish a higher purchase price upon which any future capital appreciation will build; thus mitigating eventual CGT liabilities.

It is generally useful to carry over into the UK any assets showing a loss since not only can losses be used as an offset against future CGT assessments but unless professionally advised otherwise there is no real point in disposing of an asset which might in future increase in value.

Remember that once considered resident for UK tax purposes you may also use the indexed sum [currently £6,300] beneath which no CGT is levied.

You must also not forget that the profits from the sale of foreign property might be liable to CGT as might profits from trading in currencies; there is a great deal to think about when the UK tax implications of returning to the UK permanently [or even briefly, sometimes]. Do your thinking out loud with a qualified adviser's ear available. It simply is not practical to "bed and breakfast" realty. The legal fees, stamp duties and allied costs associated with the sale and purchase of land or property will inevitably mop up any tax advantages that might have existed.

National Insurance

The social security implications of returning to the UK to resume residence do not, contrary to popular belief, run in harness with the UK tax laws. And they are quite a complicated set of regulations which have to be considered.

The short term expatriate [he to whom the "one sixth rule" applies] who has been employed abroad by a firm who has a place of business in the UK has the simplest task. Since he will have been paying Class 1 contributions throughout his stay abroad [unless he has exceeded a calendar year abroad by several months] he will, upon resuming UK based duties, simply continue the status quo.

If he has been abroad long enough to have exceeded the 52 week rule and has been eligible to pay Class 2 or Class 3 contributions voluntarily, he will be in the same category as a short term expatriate who has been working for a wholly foreign employer with no place of business in the UK. Both will begin to pay Class 1 contributions from the moment they take up duties in the UK, or will have to consult their local Social Security office if they find themselves un-employed or intend to become self employed.

The requirements to be fulfilled by any expatriate who was "not ordinarily resident" [in accordance with DHSS regulations, this time!] who, having paid his Class 3 contributions, returns to take up employment or enter self employment are similar to those I have just described. He will either immediately start paying Class 1 along with his PAYE tax deductions or be required to pay Class 2 and Class 4 if he works as a sole trader.

The only other category, the "I've-had-enough-of-this-lark-and-don't-want-to-see-another-bloody-foreigner-I'm-going-to-grow-grapes-in-Sussex-and-retire-at-50" man [who seems to be very much in evidence amongst expatriates who have amassed more than £75,000 in capital, poor soon-to-be-disillusioned-souls] should consult his local Social Security office too.

He should at least pay Class 3 contributions towards his State pension until boredom [which may take a month or two of watching afternoon TV to set in] or the realisation that only a parsimonious monk can retire at 50 on £75,000 [probably after two visits to the pub where he will see the price of a pint and a packet of cigarettes].

Life assurance policies

If, prior to going to work abroad you held life policies which were eligible for income tax relief on the premiums [new policies are not, now-a-days] then, now you are returning to resume residence you should inform the assurance company involved so that they may re-instate you as eligible to receive the deduction of relief which you were not entitled to whilst non-resident.

Wills

While you are discussing all these points with your adviser include mention of your will, especially if you only have one which was altered to take account of Capital Transfer Tax [1974] and which has not been changed in the light of the recently introduced Inheritance Tax. Discuss even longer and harder the point of wills if you haven't got one.

A final word

Over the past decade or so I have been accused of being cynical, unfeeling, unsympathetic and, by some, downright rude about expatriates. Since I earn part of my living giving them advice it would seem that I am expected to agree with many of the hare-brained schemes they concoct over a glass of "flash" or whatever.

One reviewer of another book of mine [next in line for a new edition] described me as "a gourmet nibbling on the hands that feed him".

My Mum told me all about sticks and stones so I take little notice; I do admit to being cynical [it is one of the ways that I manage to remain just the right side of sane] but I am not unsympathetic.

I am a working British expatriate myself and saw fifty pass three years ago. I would love to think before the next milestone in my ageing process is reached I could give up work or even slow down to a fast gallop. But I must not; I must be realistic. So too must expatriates of my generation; I say, and shall continue to say, that anyone who expects to live off the income produced [after tax] from £75,000 from now to the age of seventy five, to provide for his widow, account for inflation and the other "nasties" of life [such as buying a pair of shoes] is kidding himself to a degree bordering on masochism.

Throughout this book I have pleaded, nagged and threatened you about the need to take professional advice all along the line. I have told you of the consequences of trying to wrong foot the tax man when you yourself are standing on one leg upon fast shifting sands.

I have warned you about letting salesmen sell you too much life assurance when what you probably need is life insurance; I have argued against your investing in anything until you have tucked away some "fall back" capital into a bank or building society account. I have tried to worry you about leasing your home to total strangers without the proper protection afforded you by the Rent Act.

There must be an easier way for me to earn a living! But I enjoy doing what I am doing albeit that once in a while [like once every ten minutes!] I wonder why I am doing it.

There comes a time when the pleading, the nagging, the threatening and the warnings have to stop.

If you are reading these final few lines preparatory to going home I wish you well.

I hope that you are satisfied with what you have achieved working abroad; that constant travel, occasional tummy bugs, strange foods, smells and sounds, and long absences from your family and friends have not made life too uncomfortable and that you feel, with at least a measure of self satisfaction, you having done what you could as well as you knew how, you can now go home.

That is where I am going.

THE LAST THING ONE DISCOVERS IN WRITING A BOOK, IS WHAT TO PUT FIRST.

WORKING ABROAD?
Reader Enquiry Service

To find out more about the services of any advertiser in this edition of "Working Abroad?" simply complete this card and send it to the address shown overleaf. Your details will then be forwarded to the advertisers you choose.

- ☐ Aurigny Air Services
- ☐ Barclay Unicorn International
- ☐ Commercial Bank of Wales
- ☐ ERC — International Selection
- ☐ Fidelity International
- ☐ Gabbitas-Thring
- ☐ Hill Samuel & Co [Jersey] Ltd
- ☐ Jardine Fleming Investment
- ☐ MediCare
- ☐ NatWest Special Reserve
- ☐ Save & Prosper Group
- ☐ Shannon Kneale [Accountants]
- ☐ Tyndall Fund Managers
- ☐ Wingspan Travellers Club
- ☐ Banner Overseas Financial Services
- ☐ Britannia International Management
- ☐ Dunning & Co [Solicitors]
- ☐ Errolgrange Insurance Group
- ☐ Freemans International
- ☐ Guernsey Tourist Board
- ☐ LLoyds Bank Finance [Jersey] Ltd
- ☐ Midland Bank Trust Corporation
- ☐ Robeco
- ☐ School Fees Insurance Agency
- ☐ Trustee Savings Bank
- ☐ Unilife Assurance
- ☐ York House Financial Services

If you have any other areas of interest simply indicate them by ticking the appropriate box below. Your interest will be indicated to any future advertiser in EXPATXTRA! who offers services in these areas. If you use this facility you could receive a great deal of mail.

- ☐ Banking [Off-shore]
- ☐ Building Society Accounts
- ☐ Gift services
- ☐ Investment advice
- ☐ Investment Funds [off-shore]
- ☐ Life assurance
- ☐ Medical insurance
- ☐ Mediterranean Properties
- ☐ Pension plans
- ☐ School fees
- ☐ Tax counselling
- ☐ Travel
- ☐ UK car hire
- ☐ UK investment property

BLOCK CAPITALS PLEASE

NAME ....

ADDRESS ....

....

....

WORKING ABROAD?
Reader Enquiry Service

To find out more about the services of any advertiser in this edition of "Working Abroad?" simply complete this card and send it to the address shown overleaf. Your details will then be forwarded to the advertisers you choose.

- ☐ Aurigny Air Services
- ☐ Barclay Unicorn International
- ☐ Commercial Bank of Wales
- ☐ ERC — International Selection
- ☐ Fidelity International
- ☐ Gabbitas-Thring
- ☐ Hill Samuel & Co [Jersey] Ltd
- ☐ Jardine Fleming Investment
- ☐ MediCare
- ☐ NatWest Special Reserve
- ☐ Save & Prosper Group
- ☐ Shannon Kneale [Accountants]
- ☐ Tyndall Fund Managers
- ☐ Wingspan Travellers Club
- ☐ Banner Overseas Financial Services
- ☐ Britannia International Management
- ☐ Dunning & Co [Solicitors]
- ☐ Errolgrange Insurance Group
- ☐ Freemans International
- ☐ Guernsey Tourist Board
- ☐ LLoyds Bank Finance [Jersey] Ltd
- ☐ Midland Bank Trust Corporation
- ☐ Robeco
- ☐ School Fees Insurance Agency
- ☐ Trustee Savings Bank
- ☐ Unilife Assurance
- ☐ York House Financial Services

If you have any other areas of interest simply indicate them by ticking the appropriate box below. Your interest will be indicated to any future advertiser in EXPATXTRA! who offers services in these areas. If you use this facility you could receive a great deal of mail.

- ☐ Banking [Off-shore]
- ☐ Building Society Accounts
- ☐ Gift services
- ☐ Investment advice
- ☐ Investment Funds [off-shore]
- ☐ Life assurance
- ☐ Medical insurance
- ☐ Mediterranean Properties
- ☐ Pension plans
- ☐ School fees
- ☐ Tax counselling
- ☐ Travel
- ☐ UK car hire
- ☐ UK investment property

BLOCK CAPITALS PLEASE

NAME ....

ADDRESS ....

....

....

AIRMAIL

Affix
postage
here

READER SERVICES
PO BOX 300
JERSEY
CHANNEL ISLANDS

AIRMAIL

Affix
postage
here

READER SERVICES
PO BOX 300
JERSEY
CHANNEL ISLANDS

It was never my intention to produce an index; vain-gloriously hoping as I was, that you would want to read every word in the order in which I had written them. Greater forces than I — such as publishers and booksellers — have prevailed.

Ungraciously I have succumbed to the idea that this book will sell better if I include one and to the practical point that it is my bank balance rather than my ego that needs boosting.

Nevertheless, I hope that you will only use the following pages to refresh your memory as to where nuggets of information might be found rather than simply to look up matters which you think might apply to you.

Unless you are a very unusual working British expatriate you will have need to read everything rather than pick out morsels. Information, like food, taken at the gallop is inclined to cause indigestion. I therefore encourage you, even beg you, to take the book as a whole meal. There are sufficient in-built laxatives to prevent you becoming constipated.

Harry Brown

INDEX

USEFUL ADDRESSES

BBC External Services
Bush House
Strand
London WC1

Blair Consular Services Ltd
10 Fairfield Avenue
Staines, Middlesex [Visas and permits]

British Association of Removers
279 Gray's Inn Road
London WC1

Braham Masters & Co Ltd
Staplehurst Road
Sittingbourne, Kent [Packing & Overseas Removals]

Giltspur Bullens Transport Services Ltd
408 Hornsey Road
London N19 ,, ,,

Neale Wilkinson Ltd
78 Stratford Broadway
London E15 ,, ,,

Trans Euro
Second Way
Wembley
Middlesex ,, ,,

Country Cousins Courier Service
6 Springfield Road
Horsham
West Sussex RH12 2PB [Courier Services]

DHL International [UK] Ltd
Kings House
Great West Road
Brentford, Middlesex ,, ,,

British Medical Association
BMA House
Tavistock Square
London WC1H 9JP

Department of Health & Social Security
Overseas Branch
Benton Park Road
Newcastle upon Tyne NE98 1YX
[deals with contributions whilst abroad]

Department of Health & Social Security
Information Division
Leaflets Unit
Block 4 Government Building
Honeypot Lane, Stanmore, Middlesex
[deals with DHSS publications]

British Airways Medical Unit
75 Regent Street
London W1 [Vaccinations]

British Caledonian Airways Medical Unit
London Airport — Gatwick
Horley, Surrey ,, ,,

Thomas Cook Vaccination Centre
45 Berkeley Square
London W1 ,, ,,

Any County Medical Officer will advise the nearest centre for vaccinations outside London

"Travellers Health"
by Dr. Richard Dawood
published by Oxford University Press
ISBN 0-19-261562-9
available from most book shops [£6.95]

International Planned Parenthood Federation
18-20 Lower Regent Street
London SW1Y 4PW [Contraceptive advice]

Personnel International Ltd
P O Box 240
St Peter Port
Guernsey, Channel Islands [Counselling: Foreign Employment]

Professional & Executive Recruitment Overseas
4-5 Grosvenor Place
London SW1X 7SB ,, ,,

European Council of International Schools
18 Lavant Street
Petersfield
Hampshire GU32 3EW [Education advice]

Gabbitas-Thring Educational Trust
Broughton House
6 Sackville Street
London W1X 2BR ,, ,,

Independent Schools Information Service
26 Caxton Street
London SW1H 0RG ,, ,,

Truman Knightley Educational Trust
76-78 Notting Hill Gate
London W11 3LJ ,, ,,

World-Wide Education Service
Strode House
44-50 Osnaburgh Street
London NW1 3NN ,, ,,

Open University
Student Enquiry Service
P O Box 71
Bletchley, Bucks

Pitmans Correspondence College
Worcester Road
Wimbledon SW19

The British Council
90-91 Tottenham Court Road
London W1P 0DT

The Centre for International Briefing
Farnham Castle
Farnham, Surrey GU9 0AG [Briefing & Counselling]

Women's Corona Society
Room 501
Eland House
Stag Place
London SW1E 5DH ,, ,,

The EXPATRIATE
25 Brighton Road
South Croydon CR2 6EA [monthly publication]

EXPATXTRA!
P O Box 300
Jersey, Channel Islands [monthly publication]

Home and Away
62 Tritton Road
London SE20 8DE ,, ,,

Resident Abroad
102-108 Clerkenwell Road
London WC1B 3PP ,, ,,

Royal Commonwealth Society
18 Northumberland Avenue
London WC2 [Country Guides]

International Society for the Protection of Animals
106 Jermyn Street
London SW1 [Animal care]

RSPCA
Causeway
Horsham
Sussex ,, ,,

Spratt's Patent Ltd
Central House
Cambridge Road
Barking, Essex ,, ,,

INDEX OF ADVERTISERS

To receive details about the services offered by any advertiser in this edition of Working Abroad? you may use one of the cards incorporated and return it to Reader Services, P O Box 300, Jersey, Channel Islands.

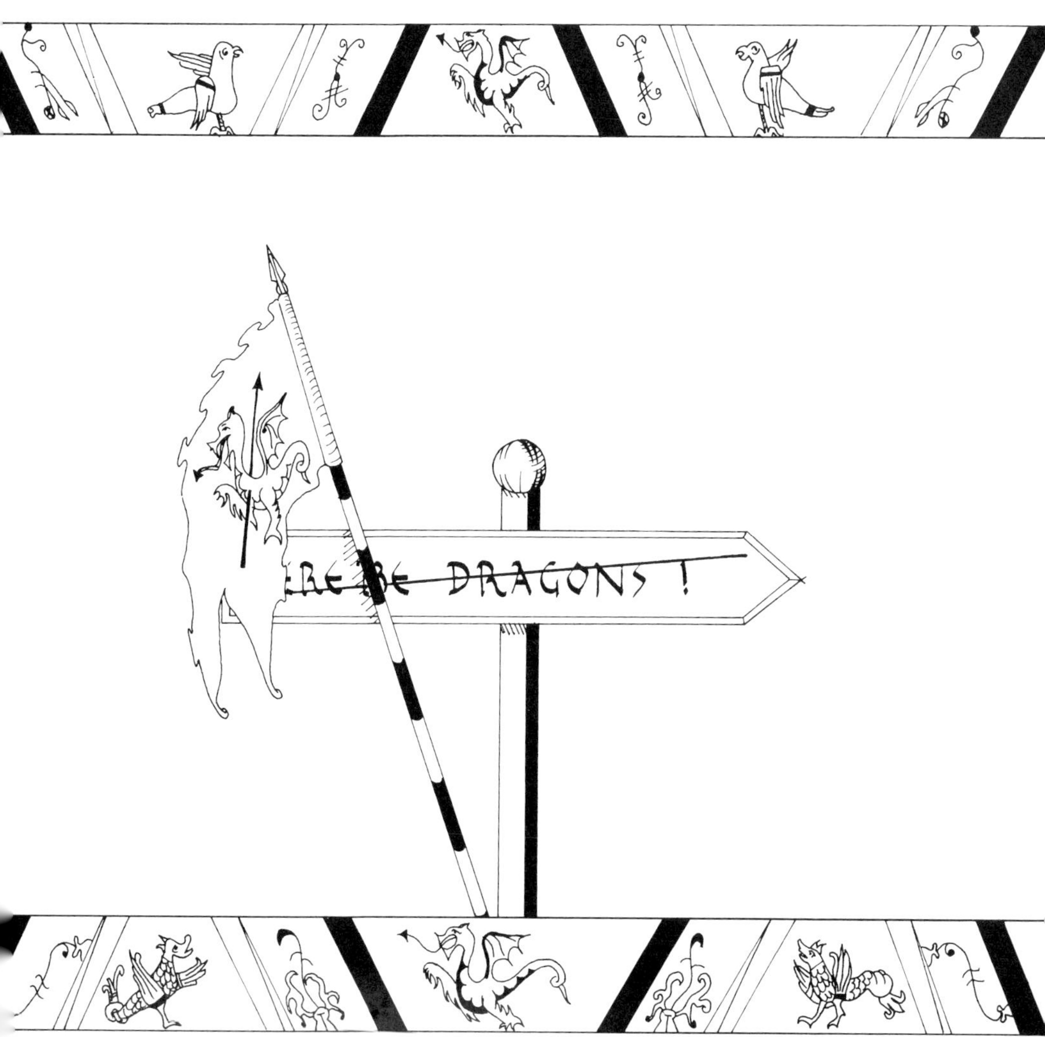
ere Be DRAGONS !

Also available from Northcote House

For Parents and Students

The Gabbitas-Thring Guide to Independent Further Education

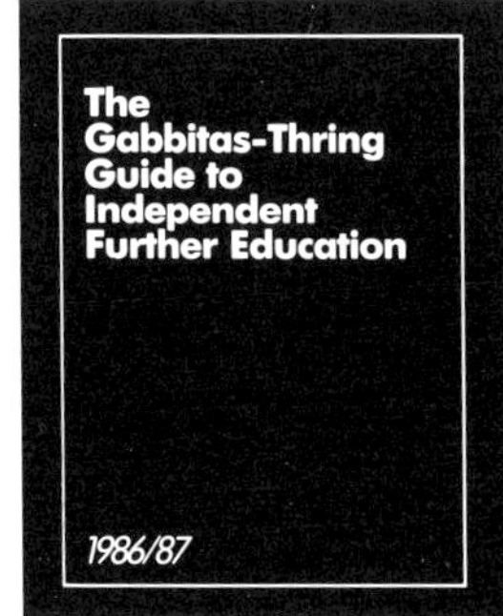

Gabbitas-Thring, the world renowned educational advisory trust, with over 100 years experience in the field of education, provides parents, teachers, careers advisers and students with the first really comprehensive source book on the growing independent sector in British Education today. With more than 600 detailed entries and informative articles by leading specialist contributors, this new *Guide* meets a real need for objective consumer information on private Schools, Colleges and Training Establishments in all areas of Further Education from GCE and secretarial to technical and domestic arts and as such, will provide an invaluable new reference source for everyone concerned with the highest standards in Further Education.
192pp, 254 x 190mm. Illustrated.
£9.95 paperback. 0 7463 0388 2.
£15.00 hardback. 0 7463 0393 9.

For Investors

Accountants Guide to the European Communities

Dennis Evans

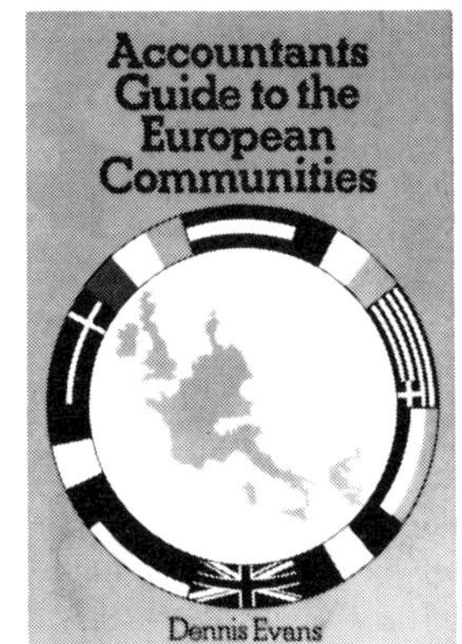

A much needed practical guide to the political, economic and financial institutions of the EEC and its member states. Contents: introduction, organisation and management of the Community, economics and monetary union, budgets, the company in Europe, the accountant in Europe, general policies of the Community, educational and research facilities, appendices, index. Foreword by Roy Jenkins. "There is certainly more than enough in the book to give the reader a . . . better understanding of its policies and institutions." *British Book News,* 1981.
384pp, 234 x 156mm.
£22.50 hardback. 0 7121 0156 X.

Also available from Northcote House

Banking Dictionary German/English-English/German

Hans Klaus

This book contains translations and short definitions (in German and English) of banking terms, and familiarises the user with Swiss, British and American banking terminology. This fifth edition (1984) has been brought fully up to date in the light of specialist reference works, bank brochures and newspaper articles. It will be an essential purchase for all those concerned with international banking, investment, brokerage, finance, taxation, securities, economics, and commercial law.
1984. *234pp, 208 x 103mm. 5th edition.*
£15.00 paperback. 0 7121 5626 7.

Glossary of Financial and Economic Terms

C. A. Gunston & H. Zahn

A substantial aid for interpreters, translators and correspondents in foreign trade, commerce, finance, banking and government. It includes terms relating to company annual accounts and reports, investment analysis, building society and instalment finance, insurance, shipping, average adjustment and international litigation with a financial slant. "This dictionary will have an assured readership." *Accountants Magazine.*
German/English: 1,288pp, 190 x 125mm. £43.00 hardback.
0 7121 5474 4.
English/German: 530pp, 190 x 125mm. £35.50 hardback.
0 7121 5475 2.
2nd edition 1982.
Supplement £2.00. 0 7121 5495 7.

Leading European Banks 1982

Kurt Tritten

An authoritative study of leading European banks — their individual size, productivity and profitability. An essential aid to corporate meetings where financial policy objectives are to be defined. This will be an indispensable book for bank executives, international research institutes, investment companies, fiduciary and consultant firms. 1982. *328pp, 210 x 160mm. 8th edition.*
£48.50 hardback. 0 7121 5615 1.